Introduction

I0845709

 Max Stirner, John Henry Mackay, James L Walker, Benjamin Tucker, Emma Goldman, Renzo Novatore, Dora Marsden, Sidney Parker; and now: Alexander Hope and the EUI.

Untouched and unwanted by the dominant neoliberal and reformed communist countries of the last 150 years, egoism has been pushed into niche corners of history and society, only being well known in certain anarchist circles, mostly leftist circles; and of course, by the practising egoists of the modern day, of which I've met, none has been more dedicated or suited to continue egoist theory than Alexander Hope.

Egoism is the taking of ownership over oneself and the world around you as your own property, and the abolition of any constructs that subvert the individual's self-interest for that of a higher power's. Many like to claim the defining feature of egoism is consciousness, the acceptance of self-interest as an individual's driving force, that makes one an egoist; but this isn't what makes someone egoist, it's merely an indicator of a type of egoist, the conscious egoist. You see, every individual, and even the great constructs (the holy ideas sustained only by their proponents forcing conditioned ideas into the material world, acting as pawns for their great immaterial overlords) such as church, nation, and capital, are all egoists inherently: they are all unique entities that, first and foremost, seek to further their own interest.

That is the defining feature of the egoist: a unique being that owns itself and as a consequence of that, and the material conditions it exists under: naturally seeks to further its own cause. Though egoism has been suppressed, kept a secret by the powers that be, lest it be used against them, Hope illustrates through the manifesto that, through necessity rather than a miraculous revival of interest of Stirner's ideas, it will indeed be egoism that reigns supreme as the final stage of history, the state of things where the fabled history of the human race and its great causes are exchanged for the fulfilling tales of great personal histories of unique individuals.

Hope does not haphazardly add on to egoism, all his assertions on egoism are based in the work of Stirner himself, or in the work of other great egoists such as Novatore and Marsden. Hope, in egoist fashion, appropriates from multiple sources, both Marxist and egoist, to present a synthesis of the two that remains consistent with both; every claim made throughout the book can be traced back to a quote by the egoists or Marxists, Hope merely assembles the pieces in a way that, to my knowledge, hasn't been yet; but nonetheless, remains consistent with itself throughout.

Hope's theories of the future view automation as the next great catalyst of history, and the next great revolution. Hope's visions of how the powers that be will handle this coming revolution are less that optimistic; to give a drastic oversimplification: under capitalism, the power of automation, instead of being used for public welfare, will only be used for profit; the labour power of the worker will plummet in favour of automated labour, which a new class of bourgeoise, the atomist bourgeoise, will be selling as a commodity to the industrial bourgeoisie. Under communism, automation will be used for public welfare, gradually lowering the need for the proletariat to labour and creating a new class of lazy idlers who appropriate the goods of society without contributing.

This slowly becomes unsustainable, and will eventually lead to a conflict between the idlers, who seek to destroy communism and replace it with a system of personal ownership; and the workers, who seek to maintain communism, but cannot do so without resurrecting the state and thus socialism. I know this book will have many communists claiming that communism is perfectly capable of surviving the Automative Revolution, that this is actually the goal, what they've hoped for: free appropriation without any labour required.

These communists may well need to study the ideas they proclaim, it is illustrated throughout this book that communism and automation are incompatible, communism rests on labour and the establishment of public property, however, the Automative Revolution would displace property relations and labour by empowering the idlers, who take freely and give nothing; which was no doubt already a problem inherent in communism, but these class antagonisms are amplified by the conditions of the Automative Revolution. In a true stateless, classless, moneyless society, any attempt to create a system or institution to limit the free appropriation of goods would alter communism's character into something else, as it would be incompatible with the principle of "From each according to their ability, to each according to their need." We egoists agree that the merging of communism and automation is the next step in the development of "humanity," we simply disagree that the synthesis of this merger could still be called communism. Neither capitalism, socialism, or communism have safety nets in place and neither are prepared for the coming crises, neither of them can survive them; it will become clear that egoism is the only solution.

This book mainly deals with the scenario in which the higher stage of communism described by Karl Marx has been achieved (stateless, classless, moneyless). The EUI intends on releasing works covering how the Automative Revolution will affect other economic systems in more detail, but that is not part of the core of this text; The Union remains assured however, that whatever the case, egoism will emerge as the final stage of 'humanity,' assuming humanity doesn't burn itself up with atomic fireballs or global temperatures first that is. The most likely outcome of pre-communist systems encountering the Automative Revolution would be the acceleration of those systems into communism, and then egoism. The Automative Revolution would transform capitalism into socialism, and socialism into communism. The purpose of the Idler's Revolution is to provide a means, for those who seek it, to take a portion of the means of production for themselves to own directly for their own needs and wants, rather than the productive forces being owned by an abstraction such as society as a whole, or bourgeois private property laws. This first edition was finished during a very busy time for the Union, and has thus been released without its planned annotations or accompanying writings to meet its deadline. This first edition is only being released in a limited number, and additions to the main body of text are still being considered, if anyone has questions, or suggestions, or would otherwise like to contact the Union, send an email to euitnchapter@gmail.com There are two major takeaways that could arise from this text, one is a literal interpretation and outline for the revolutionaries of the future, and the other is a more metaphorical interpretation of the ideological triumph of egoism over the spectre of ideology. And then there are those who see this text as neither sacred nor mere idealism, take the conclusions of the manifesto as tools in their own arsenal, and find it in their will to act on the ideas and bring the theory to life. Those that have chosen the third path have assembled into the Egoist Union International. This group, founded by Hope, myself, and a few key others, serves now as a free association of like-minded egoists, writing and spreading egoist literature and art, helping one another where our interests align and providing an alternative mode of support and association, an imprint of the union of egoists to come, a model out of which the modes of the future will spring from, and a safe haven in the modern day allowing members to take some reprieve from their current exploitative systems and rely less on them. In its current state, the union serves as a lower stage vanguard for the coming revolution of automation. In the future, when certain necessary factors out of the Union's control begin to unfold, the union will be prepared to take a higher stage of vanguardism over the revolution.

The German philosopher Max Stirner is the core behind this manifesto. Stirner's magnum opus, *The Unique and Its Property,* or as known in German, *Der Einzige und sein Eigenthum,* presents the highest iconoclasm. Nothing more radical than what Stirner put forth could be imagined, thought, put into words or action. This manifesto does not offer an improvement or evolution to Stirner's ideas, but rather, an application of his thinking to our modern society in a manner that is completely new and Unique. This is the only innovation we offer; the mere reality that we are living in another time.

The Idler's Manifesto is a call to arms for all those who refuse to be devalued by the state. It is an invitation to forsake the paths of imposed morality and legality, to reclaim individual value, and to witness the withering of the state. Together, as unique egoists, we stand not as beggars, but as individuals of inherent worth. Let us embrace our idleness, transform our pauperism, and rise as the true masters of our own destiny.

''Salvation is amusing to saviours, and we would not remonstrate with them, having no desire to spoil fun: and few things provide as much good sport as a good cause! We merely endeavour to give the tip to the quarry: to the people who are in danger of being saved, and it is 'Don't refuse to be dealt with!' It is a matter we cannot enlarge upon her, but it is the gist of the gospel of power to those who would be free men'' - Dora Marsden, 1914, The Egoist, p.162.

"I dream of a world in which I would be guillotined as a conservative" - Pierre Joseph Proudhon

- Alexander Hope with an Introduction by Erik Bonhomme

The Idler's Manifesto

A spectre is haunting the world—the spectre of Pauperism. All the powers of the old social order, from the Imperialist Communist International of the fractured Soviet-aligned countries, to the American bourgeoisie and the decayed European Union, have joined in a holy alliance to exorcise this spook. The Italian egoist Novatore similarly remarked in his *Towards the Creative Nothing* that 'The bourgeois and proletarian, though clashing over questions of class, of power, and of the belly, still always remained united in common hatred against the great vagabonds of the spirit, against the solitaries of the idea, against all those stricken by thought, against all those transfigured by a superior beauty.' He continued, 'Only the great vagabonds of the idea can—and must—be the luminous spiritual fulcrum of the tempestuous revolution, which advances in gloom upon the world.' The humane bourgeoisie and communists alike harbour a great hatred toward the egoist.

Stirner, being further ahead of the curtain of history, remarked that 'Criticism and the masses pursue the same goal, freedom from egoism, and wrangle only over which of them approaches nearest to the goal or even attains it. The Jews, the Christians, the absolutists, the men of darkness and men of light, politicians, communists—all, in short—hold the reproach of egoism far from them; and, as criticism brings against them this reproach in plain terms and in the most extended sense, all justify themselves against the accusation of egoism, and combat—egoism, the same enemy with whom criticism wages war. Both criticism and masses are enemies of egoists, and both seek to liberate themselves from egoism, as well by clearing or whitewashing themselves as by ascribing it to the opposite party.' The décadent philosophies of resentment are hereby easily exposed, for they are all exponents of slave morality—Judaism, Christianity, Buddhism, Liberalism, Marxism, etc. Why do these parties always fail to last?

We harken back to Max Stirner, who asked that same question: 'Why do certain opposition parties fail to flourish? Solely for the reason that they refuse to forsake the path of morality or legality.' Henceforth, let us forsake the path of morality or legality in all affairs, whether party affairs or personal affairs. Where is the party in opposition that has not been decried as egoistic by its opponents in power? Where is the opposition that has not hurled back the branding reproach of egoism against the more advanced opposition parties, as well as against its reactionary adversaries?

Two things result from this fact:

Egoism was, is, and always will be in itself a power that is constantly acknowledged as a power throughout all of world history.

It is high time that egoists should openly, in the face of the whole world, publish their views, their aims, and their tendencies and meet the nursery tale of the Specter of Pauperism with a Manifesto of its Union.

To this end, egoists have assembled in unique corners of the world to sketch the following manifesto. The idlers of the world may be viewed as good as nothing else but beggars on the street but Satan finds some mischief for idle hands to do.

I. SERF-PROLETARIANS AND IDLERS

'History, hitherto, is the history of the intellectual man.' After the period of sensuality, history proper begins: the period of intellectuality, spirituality, supersensuality, nonsensicality. Man, now begins to want to be and become something. What? Good, beautiful, true; more precisely, moral, pious, agreeable, etc. He wants to make of himself a 'proper man,' - 'something proper.' Man is his goal, his ought, his destiny, calling, task, his—ideal: he is to himself a future, other-worldly he. And what makes a 'proper fellow' of him? Being true, being good, being moral, and the like. Now he looks askance at everyone who does not recognize the same 'what,' seek the same morality, have the same faith; he chases out 'separatists, heretics, sects.' This is precisely the history of class struggle whereby one class asserts itself over another and, because it does not share its same faith, chases the other class out as a deviationist from the correct party line, as heretic, eclectic, separatist, mechanical vulgar materialist, utopian, petit-bourgeois, idealist, metaphysician, chauvinistic, comprador, class traitor, adventurist, reformist, counter-revolutionary, revisionist, reactionary, dogmatist or warlordist, sabotagist, right opportunist, capitulator liquidationist, etc, until it is completely vanquished and beaten. Therefore, we might also unequivocally say that the history of the intellectual man is also 'the history of all hitherto existing societies' which, in the penultimate analysis, is 'the history of class struggle.' All of this culminates in my own struggle, which is of the highest importance to me. The final analysis of history that overcomes this penultimate analysis is merely 'that the individual is of himself a world's history and possesses his property in the rest of the world's history, goes beyond what is Christian, and subsequently goes beyond what is socialist or communist.

Freeman, slave, and sluggard; patrician, plebeian, and monk; lord, serf, and almsman; guild-master, journeyman, and vagabond; peasant, nobility, and sans-culotte; bourgeois, proletariat, and lumpenproletariat—in a word, the oppressor, the oppressed, and the undesirable stood in constant opposition to one another, carried on an uninterrupted, now hidden, now open fight; a fight which each time ended either in a revolutionary reconstitution of society, or in the common ruin of the contending classes. The undesirable class has always been a class that found itself swaying towards allegiances with property owners or workers for its own survival. In other words, idlers possess elements from both the oppressors and the oppressed. For the longest time, the idlers have been considered the dung of society, 'that passively rotting mass thrown off by the lowest layers of the old society.' As idlers have the power to be oppressed or oppress others, idlers are ultimately absorbed into one class or another in proxy struggles of other social classes. When they finally learn to struggle as a unified class for their own desires without being absorbed into other alien struggles, they will eventually take the first step towards egoism and leave behind their vagabond past.

In the earlier epochs of history, we find almost everywhere a complicated arrangement of society into various orders, a manifold gradation of social rank. In primitive history, we have freemen, sluggards and hunter-gatherers. In ancient Rome we had patricians, plebeians, slaves; in the Middle Ages, feudal lords, vassals, guild-masters, journeymen, apprentices, serfs, vagabonds; in almost all of these classes, again, subordinate gradations. In bourgeois society we have, the bourgeoisie, the industrial proletariat and the lumpenproletariat. The socialism of the 20th century further developed the industrial proletariat, until China and the USSR eventually adopted a Kruschev-Dengist model of revisionism which merged the unholy forces of socialism and capitalism.

The communist society of the future will sprout from the ruins of bourgeois society. Modern communist society will not do away with class antagonisms; it will, and already has, but established new classes; new conditions of oppression, new forms of struggle in place of the old ones. The epoch of communism, like the previous epoch of capitalism, will simplify class struggle into two camps, two great classes directly facing each other: Serf-Proletariat and Idler. From the dispossessed peasants of the Middle Ages sprang the chartered guildsmen and journeymen of the earliest towns. From these guildsmen and journeymen, the first elements of the industrial proletariat were developed.

Now as to the question, what is the serf-proletariat? The serf-proletariat is an echo of the decay of both feudalism and capitalism. In capitalism, the lumpenproletariat was the result of the decay of the old society, in communism the opposite is true. The idlers are created as a direct consequence of the serf-proletarian's existence. The serf-proletariat is quite simply the result of the decay of two regimes: That of feudalism and capitalism. The industrial proletariat becomes a serf-proletariat when it can see itself in direct antagonism with the idler in a communist society that has been more or less achieved. Friedrich Engels in his book, *The Principles of Communism* describes the character of the proletariat and the serf in the following paragraph:

'The serf possesses and uses an instrument of production, a piece of land, in exchange for which he gives up a part of his product or part of the services of his labour. The proletarian works with the instruments of production of another, for the account of this other, in exchange for a part of the product. The serf gives up, the proletarian receives. The serf has an assured existence, the proletarian has not. The serf is outside competition, the proletarian is in it. The serf liberates himself in one of three ways: either he runs away to the city and there becomes a handicraftsman; or, instead of products and services, he gives money to his lord and thereby becomes a free tenant; or he overthrows his feudal lord and himself becomes a property owner. In short, by one route or another, he gets into the owning class and enters into competition. The proletarian liberates himself by abolishing competition, private property, and all class differences.'

We can also remark that, the serf-proletarian of communism, like the serf of the Middle Ages, possesses and uses an instrument of production, the land, in exchange for which he gives up not just part of his services of labour and product, but all of his product and services of labour to society at large. The only defining quality of the serf-proletariat is that he owns the means of production rather than merely using and possessing them as if he owned them.

The serf-proletariat, like the industrial proletariat, labours for another (society at large) and for the account of this other, and in exchange, receives part of the product according to his needs. The serf-proletarian has to both give up and receive because he can be best described in character as a conglomeration of the feudal serf and the industrial proletariat. The serf-proletarian both has assured existence while also not having this assured existence if he were to become an idler. The serf-proletariat is both within competition and outside it. He is in competition because of the idler's exploitation of his surplus value, and he is outside of it because he himself cannot compete in any way against the idler. The serf-proletarian can liberate himself in a number of ways: either he runs away from the cities and becomes an idler; or instead of providing needs to society freely, the serf-proletarian decides to unite together to rebuild a state apparatus in order to hand out the wealth of society through currency in such a manner that will halt the free appropriation of all goods and revert society back to socialism. The last manner for the serf-proletariat to free itself is to become an idler revolutionary, to overthrow the serf-proletarian state machinery, and utilise it to change the mode of production into an egoistic mode of production. The industrial proletariat by one short route or another gets into the owning class and enters into partitioning. The Unique liberates itself by abolishing partitioning, public property, and all class differences.

The serf-proletariat, because he is in competition with the idler, starts to reorganise the socialist state machinery in order to extinguish this new class that is destroying communist society. The serf-proletariat, in order to regress back to the worker's state, has to also destroy elements of communist society itself, such as the partitioning of goods according to one's needs and public property. The new dictatorship of the serf-proletariat will replace partitioning according to one's needs with wage-slavery under socialistic conditions, and transform public property back into state property. In other words, the serf-proletariat resumed what was clear to see in the Soviet Union of the past, with the means of production under state property and wage-slavery under fairer socialistic conditions. In other words, they reintroduce a clear form of currency and intensify class struggle between the idler and the labourer with the further destabilisation of communist society as a whole. When communist society regresses back to the socialist state with a government - that government is also in danger of potential revisionists within it, ones that may want to privatise industry and return all the way again back to the ancient regime of liberal capitalism. These potential revisionists we call the petit-bourgeois serfs can transform themselves into the resurrected Automative Bourgeoise that spread further revisionism, small outburst of capitalist restoration within revisionist socialist worker's states of the serf-proletarians. Revisionists often at first attack subtly by using dogmatism or justify their attacks against "extremism." Revisionists triumph by disturbing democratic centralism and the discussion process. They use their elaborate phraseology to justify their bourgeoisie stance within the party. In the scenario hereby explored, the serf-proletarian dictatorship might have three particular views: 'Either to defeat idlers by progressing forward into communism once again, a neutral position whereby state socialism is seen as the only eternal remedy to the problem of the idler, and lastly, the most revisionist position, is to restore capitalism piece by piece in such a way that can defeat the idlers' - For the idler class, any method that is utilised in order to defeat their evolution and empowerment as a class is inherently reactionary and revisionist. There are degrees of revisionism, that is to say some are more revisionist than others. The restoration of socialism that is slowly decaying communism is seen as a revisionist movement by the idler and even some labourers themselves who feel as if they were betrayed by the other serf-proletarians in contributing to the overall destruction of the communist society which after all, proletarians themselves have built.

Communism, far from being a stable society, is really an unstable society attacked from various fronts. That being said, before going into detail why precisely communism is an unstable economic system, we must go over a brief history of 20th century socialism.

The Bolshevik revolution opened up fresh ground for the rising industrial proletariat. Its social imperialism had spread far and wide as it traded with its enemy; the bourgeoisie. The rapid growth of the means of production in semi-feudal countries transformed them into socialist countries. The capitalist system of industry which was monopolised by its finance aristocracy was no longer sufficient for the growing wants of the socialist state. The bourgeoisie were pushed on one side by the manufacturing proletarian class; division of labour between the different corporate monopolies vanished in the face of division of labour by the proletarians through the state. In the meantime, the dictatorship of the proletariat kept growing; the demand for labour was ever rising. The old semi-feudal workshops and manufacture no longer sufficed. Thereupon, the dictatorship of the proletariat had to invest its labours in the construction of heavy industrial machinery to revolutionise its industrial production; the place of manufacture was taken from the hands of the bourgeoisie by the proletariat. Modern industry had established a social market for which the USSR paved the way, this social arrangement had the proletariat sell his labour without contract to the dictatorship of the proletariat, and in exchange, receive a wage. This was an immense development for commerce and what once was called the private capital of the bourgeoisie, now transformed into the social capital of the state; the dictatorship of the proletariat. This social industrial capital is then utilised again in the form of money to generate even more social profit that has to be split among all members of society in the form of a pay rate, essentially acting as a wage and continuing wage labour. We see, therefore, how the modern socialist proletariat is itself the product of a series of revolutions in the modes of production and of exchange. The proletariat increased their capital and pushed into the background every class handed down from the French Revolution, the old colonial powers of the early bourgeois age. Each step in the development of the proletariat was accompanied by a corresponding political advance of that class. Numerous socialist revolutions ignited in the last century and the proletariat, historically, has played a most revolutionary part.

The proletariat, wherever it gets the upper hand, has put an end to most capitalist relations. It has torn asunder the capitalist ties that bound man to his employer, it has resolved personal exchange value into a social exchange value and has set up a conscionable tyranny: the freedom of the state. It has socialised capitalism; but it is capitalism nonetheless; until communism is achieved: a stateless, classless, moneyless society with productive forces strong enough to be able to provide for all the needs of all members of society as long as they utilise their ability to labour.

That being said, every revolution in history has faced its share of traitors and revisionists, and the Bolshevik revolution was no exception. The blending of socialism and capitalism has created a complex and often contradictory force. In particular, China exemplifies this fusion through the Kruschev-Dengist model, where both the industrial bourgeoisie and the proletariat share power within the Chinese Communist Party (CCP). This arrangement has led to a paradox: while the ruling class—comprising both the bourgeoisie and the proletariat—maintains its dominance, the lower proletariat increasingly falls into pauperism, becoming the exploited class.

The CCP now faces a critical dilemma: either it will uphold the interests of the industrial bourgeoisie and proletariat against the divisive forces of American Atomism, or it will succumb to these same divisive forces. For the purposes of this manifesto, "atomism" represents the third stage of capitalism, the highest and final stage of imperialism.

Capitalism in the 21st century has once again undergone a metamorphosis in material conditions which will ultimately cause a crisis of production that will lead to an ideological revolt of the 5th estate (Lumpenproletariat) and thus bring about the post-humanist era. The modern crisis of production is mainly being caused by the Automative Revolution which transforms the means and mode of production much more radically than previous revolutions, I.E the Digital Revolution, the Industrial Revolution and the ancient agricultural revolution. We are bearing witness to the rise of machines and artificial intelligence that can operate independently of human labour or with limited human intervention which ultimately destroys many forms of labour at a much faster rate than it can create them. It wreaks havoc on old industries, on the industrial bourgeoisie and the industrial proletariat.

This new radical revolution not only changes the materialistic "base" of human society but also its "superstructure." It does for instance cause great changes within the Marxist doctrine which sees itself evolving into Stirnerite egoism as it leaves behind socialism as a spooky ideal. Marxism was an ideology thought up and constructed with the industrial revolution in mind and with a powerful industrial proletariat at its disposal. This automated revolution decimates everything it comes into contact with - most especially the old industrial methods of production and the industrial proletariat. With the old methods of production vanquished and the powerful industrial proletarian class no longer at its disposal, Marxism can no longer challenge those classes in power. With the slow death of the working class, the industrial bourgeoisie would also surely perish and would this not also signify the death of capitalism and the birth of communism? We shall see that this is not the case, as capital, profit, exploitation, the division of labour and classes still exist only under new forms. In this case, capitalism has evolved past its own industrial limitations rather than vanished.

Marxism inevitably destroys itself through its own logic as it dialectically turns inwards into itself and supersedes itself; becoming egoism. We shall soon show how this process from Marxism to Egoism takes place but for the time being it is essential to understand that every time capitalism had evolved, Marxism had to evolve with it in order to adjust itself to the new demanding nature of imperialism. This was done several times, with Lenin, Stalin and Mao who all revised Marxism in order to meet the challenges of modern-day imperialism. Those who do not revise Marxism to answer to new material conditions are easily branded as dogmatists and worshippers of the "Book." What do you have against us when we egoists use that same Marxist spirit of revising Marxism itself to meet the new challenges of the Automative Revolution? You are only against us because we have revealed that Marxism has to once again evolve at the same rapid pace as the Automative Revolution and that we are leaving Marxism behind in exchange for Stirner's egoism. Throughout this manifesto we will follow the same scientific logic of Marxism and make use of its tools such as the notions of class struggle, an understanding of political economy, materialism, historical and dialectical materialism etc.

The Marxists will no doubt complain and state that this manifesto merely spouts bourgeois lies in bad faith, but is it really bourgeois lies when we are using your own tools of understanding and Marxist logic to reach our conclusion?

This manifesto will attempt to accomplish two monstrous tasks. We will have to firstly divide the coming future into two histories. The first history is that history which we find ourselves in the present moment. This is called the phase of atomism. In this phase, all the classes unite against the atomist bourgeoisie. This is the first history which has its own unique relations to the mode of production, capital, labour, wages, property, and so forth. We will analyse Wage Labour and Capital under this phase we call the highest stage of imperialism - Atomism. The second history comes after atomism, we call this the communist phase; that phase which comes after the lower phase of communism - namely the higher phase of communism. In this phase, the proletariat have waged a revolution and likely achieved communism, a classless, moneyless and stateless society. Although the epidemic of production remains at large in this society, the Automaton Revolution is still underway, and the idle pauper class remerges stronger than ever. It is in this phase, at the higher end of communism, that the proletariat finally becomes the serf-proletariat. The serf-proletariat does not yet come into their own in the first phase of atomism. During this second phase, for various reasons that will be explained, the class of serf-proletarians and idlers enter into a class struggle. When the idlers are at last victorious, they transition into egoists, public property becomes personal property for the egoists and society becomes the union of egoists. During this class struggle, there is a third phase, whereby the idlers take social power as the ruling class over the serf-proletariat, we call this the lower phase of egoism - this is a stage in which the egoists remain either unconscious or involuntary egoists and it is a transitory stage. The last phase of history is the higher phase of egoism - the union of egoists, where each and every egoist is at last fully conscious of his egoism and in agreement with his own voluntary egoism. For each and every one of these phases we have to analyse the relation of each class to the mode of production, to other classes, to labour, to capital, property, wage labour and the like. The conclusion of this analysis advocates for the overthrow of communist society by the lazy class (idlers) and the establishment of a union of egoists based on personal ownership of the means of production. That being said, if we are to overthrow communism, first capitalism has to be overthrown. Let us first begin with an analysis of Atomism - starting from its first phase.

II. THE PHASE OF ATOMISM AND THE PAUPER QUESTION

As the industrial revolution brought its own set of troubles, we now face new challenges with the onset of the Automative Revolution—a transformation marked by automation, self-sustaining machines and artificial intelligence. Just as Karl Marx analysed the consequences of the industrial era, it is now crucial to study how this new revolution is reshaping the mode of production, and with it, the fabric of society and its class structure.

The bourgeoisie have learned to sustain themselves as a class without relying on the proletariat having to sell their labour for a wage. The bourgeoisie could be said to have garnered the elements of the proletariat as they are now also the owners of labour, in fact, a new class has emerged, which I call the atomists. Like the ancient Greek atomists, who theorised the indivisible building blocks of matter, this class has reduced labour to its most fundamental and indivisible form: automated, machine-like labour. Atomists own and sell this automated labour as a commodity, no longer tied to human effort, but instead offered on the free market.

This shift has made automated labour the most valuable commodity of the 21st century, and atomists have accumulated immense wealth by controlling this resource. They now own factories, offices, and stores that run with minimal human intervention. The atomists are surpassing the old industrial bourgeoisie, who still rely on human labour and pay wages. As a result, the traditional proletariat, whose labour is increasingly obsolete, finds itself in a precarious position; the value of human labour has plummeted, rendering it an outdated and overpriced commodity. Why pay wages to a worker when artificial intelligence can do the same job for no ongoing cost?

The proletariat is no longer the rightful owner of his own labour and even if he does own his labour, the value of human labour is rapidly falling from his grasp. Essentially, the proletariat is the owner of a worn-out, antiquated, overpriced commodity called 'human labour' which the atomist bourgeoisie is no longer interested in purchasing.

This cold logic allows the atomists to reap far greater profits than the old bourgeoisie. In desperation, the industrial bourgeoisie might temporarily ally with the petty bourgeoisie—and even with the proletariat—to restore the old economic order, one still reliant on human labour. Yet, as automation continues to drive unemployment, both the industrial bourgeoisie and the proletariat face the same fate: a slide into pauperism, much like the aristocracy, craftsmen and rich peasants who were displaced after the French Revolution, Industrial Revolution and the subsequent Bolshevik Revolution.

Rapid industrialization, modernised imperialism and a newly evolved class of bourgeoisie are the culprit behind the rampant unemployment that we see before us. The ranks of the industrial proletariat and also the industrial bourgeoisie are being diminished and reduced to pauperism in the Automative Age.

The social question of pauperism was always of great interest to egoists, including Max Stirner himself whom according to David McLellan in his book, *The Young Hegelians and Karl Marx* claims:

Under the heading of 'Social Liberalism' Stirner next deals with — the doctrines of the communists. Whereas through the Revolution the bourgeoisie had become omnipotent and everyone was raised (or degraded) to the dignity of 'citizen,' communism or social liberalism responds:

'Our dignity and essence consist not in our being all equal children of our mother, the state, but in our all existing each for the other... that each exists only through the other who, while caring for my wants, at the same time sees his own satisfied by me. It is labour that constitutes our dignity and our equality.'

Stirner's summary of the socialist doctrine is: all must have nothing, so that all may have. Under liberalism it is what he 'has' that makes the man, and in 'having,' people are unequal. But this society where we are all to become members of the Lumpenproletariat is even worse than the previous ones, for here neither command nor property is left to the individual; the state took the former, society the latter. The communist ideas show the same faults as those already criticised. They, too, have a dualistic view of man: That the communist sees in you the man, the brother, is only the Sunday side of communism. According to the workday side he does not take you as man simply, but as human labourer or labouring man. The first view has in it the liberal principle, in the second illiberality is concealed. If you were lazy, he would certainly not fail to recognise the man in you, but would endeavour to cleanse him as a 'lazy man' from laziness and to convert him to the 'faith' that labour is man's destiny and calling. Thus, in the communists' glorification of society we merely have another in the line of deities that have tyrannised over mankind:

'Society, which is the source of all we have, is a new master, a new spook, a new "supreme being," which "takes us into its service and allegiance."'

Hence it is for this reason that Stirner views communism as yet another spook that seeks to cleanse us of our laziness, that we ought to follow our duty as the industrious, busy, laborious man. The communist recognizes my manhood but seeks to cleanse the laziness inherent in mankind, so that we may be converted to the faith of labour as our calling and destiny, but in actual fact for Stirner, I have no calling or destiny other than my own cause, the egoistic cause of my own self. Stirner therefore equates the communist doctrine with a pauper doctrine. The problem of pauperism is also the problem of communism, and any communist society of the future. Pauperism in Stirner's eyes was also the direct opposite of Stirner's concept of ego. Only when pauperism, i.e., communism, is vanquished, can the egoist reign freely.

Alexander Green in his Stirner and Marx, also argues about Stirner's contention with pauperism and communism:

'Stirner occupied a disoriented historical moment, one before the experience of capitalism and industry had been filtered through the paradigmatic Marxian idioms. Moreover, Stirner did attempt to tackle the social phenomenon of "pauperism" (the progressive impoverishment of the lower social strata) which has been identified as the "dominant" social issue of "pre-March" period. Unlike the social problems that Marx identified, pauperism was not a direct result of capitalism or even of rapid industrialization, but a problem of demographic growth and was a singularly (ignoring Berlin) rural phenomenon. Pauperism differed much from traditional poverty. It was collective and structural rather than determined by individual contingencies. Stirner recognized this social phenomenon and discussed it at length in The Ego. He was not failing to grasp the true "social question" as Marx makes out; instead, he was analysing his own reality: the parochial, yet unique, pre-Industrial phase of German history – what Eric Hobsbawn called "the last, and perhaps worst, economic breakdown of the ancien régime."'

The 21st century on the other hand has seen pauperism being caused by the rapid automation which in itself is its own pre-automation phase of history - which can easily be described as the last, and perhaps worst, economic breakdown of the bourgeois era. The modern phenomenon of pauperism can only be solved by egoism. Stirner had already suggested that egoism was a solution to the social problem of pre-industrial pauperism, he offered a definitive solution when he stated 'Pauperism can be removed only when I as ego realise value from myself, when I give my own self value, and make my price myself. I must rise in revolt to rise in the world.' which is an indication that pauperism was viewed as a problem by Stirner and it is necessary for this problem to be solved so that one may truly become a conscious and voluntary egoist.

The issue of pauperism appeared in every epoch of history under new forms and was a cause of concern for many thinkers who wrote on the issue, such as, Alexis de Tocqueville's *Memoir on Pauperism*, Karl Marx's *Pauperism and free trade: The approaching commercial crisis* and Friedrich Engels's *The Peasant War in Germany*, which concerned itself with the aforementioned peasant war generating pauperism by the thousands.

Tocqueville in particular, states something of great interest to us in his *Memoir*, that 'Man, like all socially organised beings, has a natural passion for idleness. There are, however, two incentives to work: the need to live and the desire to improve the conditions of life. Experience has proven that the majority of men can be sufficiently motivated to work only by the first of these incentives. The second is only effective with a small minority. Well, a charitable institution indiscriminately open to all those in need, or a law which gives all the poor a right to public aid, whatever the origin of their poverty, weakens or destroys the first stimulant and leaves only the second intact.' Now if the poor laws of England and charitable institution weakened or destroyed the first stimulant and left only the second intact - then a communist society, indiscriminately open to all those in need, far more advanced than a mere British Poor Law, will not only entirely destroy the first stimulant, but also destroy the second incentive;

as life under communism according to Marx has already accomplished the desire to improve the conditions of life. With the conditions of life achieving their peak under communism, and the need to live no longer an issue: man falls, like all socially organised beings, (there is nothing more socially organised than a communist society) back to their natural passion for idleness. Henceforth, pauperism would remain an issue even under this so-called future utopia. As Alexis de Tocqueville in his Memoirs on Pauperism rightfully claims 'Any measure which establishes legal charity on a permanent basis and gives it an administrative form thereby creates an idle and lazy class, living at the expense of the industrial and working class.' We egoists fully agree with Tocqueville's statement that 'the inevitable result of public charity was to perpetuate idleness among the majority of the poor and to provide for their leisure at the expense of those who work.' We egoists also argue, alongside the same lines as Tocqueville, that any future communist society as a measure to establish charity according to the needs of each person based on a permanent basis will form a lazy idler class which lives at the expense of the working class and thus a new form of struggle is born between the two classes. We have talked for a while about the issues of pauperism in a future society, should the communists actually succeed in their mission to transform all of society. Let us talk however, on the issue of pauperism in our present time, the early 21st century.

Pauperism is the greatest social problem of the 21st century, much like pauperism was the most immediate concern of the crumbling Ancien Regime. During that time of semi-feudalism, the aristocrats were in constant competition for economic dominance against the bourgeoisie. Empires such as that of Great Britain had numerous classes living side by side in a time of great confusion. Colonialism and the slave trade soon become outdated in the late 19th century, as the last of the slave traders were losing a foothold in the world and the colonies were no longer sustainable nor profitable; colonialism would eventually give way to the imperialism of the 20th century. Countries which, in the early

20th Century were still industrially backwards such as China, also had a deep problem with pauperism, so much so, that even Mao Zedong in his earliest essays mentions numerous social classes from the new world and the old-world intermingling, struggling, aiding or defeating each other. Mao Zedong in his essay, *Oppose Book Worship* counts about thirteen classes in the age of Chinese pauperism, namely the 'The Industrial proletariat, handicraft worker, farm labourers, poor peasants, urban peasants, lumpenproletariat, master handicraftsman, small merchants, middle peasants, rich peasants, land lords, commercial bourgeoisie and industrial bourgeoisie' and in his 1926 essay, *Analysis of The Classes in Chinese Society*, he writes that 'there is the fairly large lumpen-proletariat, made up of peasants who have lost their land and handicraftsmen who cannot get work.' And in comparison, the industrial proletariat numbers about two million. It is not large because China is economically backward.' And 'Though not very numerous, the industrial proletariat represents China's new productive forces' which for Mao meant that it was the most progressive class in all of China. What does this tell us? It tells us that the same thing that happened to Europe around 1789, the crumbling of the Ancien Regime and the increase of pauperism, also occurred in China around the 1920's. The problem of pauperism is once again resurfacing, as we are faced with new technologies, new revolutions in the mode of production, and new classes. The paupers, atomist bourgeoisie, atomist proletariat, atomist aristocrats, industrial bourgeoisie, industrial proletariat, lumpenproletariat, petit bourgeoisie, labour aristocrats, serf-proletarians, landlords and some other classes that fall in between are now living again side by side in a time of great confusion and upheaval much like the crumbling of the Ancien Regime.

The Atomist Bourgeoisie of the 21st century are those who act as a replacement for the industrial bourgeoisie. The atomists are those bourgeoisie that have evolved past the need of requiring the proletariat to generate profit, instead they rely solely on self-automated machinery and artificial intelligence to generate profit.

These atomist bourgeoisie are at their infancy in our own present time and we shall see their rise. The rise of the atomist bourgeoisie as a direct result of the Automative Revolution in industry presents a new challenge to traditional methods of labour agitation, such as unionism and general strikes. It shall without a doubt bring about an end to these methods, as well as bargaining power for the industrial proletariat. The movement of Labour Syndicalism becomes extinct. All workers are slowly finding themselves as part of the 'industrial reserve army' of labour; only this time, we will stay in the reserve. The increasing use of automated machinery and artificial intelligence to generate profit, coupled with the diminishing value of human labour, presents a difficult hurdle for the working class.

Even in the capitalist era of the bourgeoisie, labour is losing its inherent value. The Labour Theory of Value has become an antiquated measuring system of the ancient past. Automation is doing away with human labour as a commodity and instead robotic labour becomes the new sought out commodity. Human labour becomes disvalued, the same way vehicles made the horse and buggy useless. At this point, living labour or workers creating machines is still necessary to create any kind of surplus value. In the future, machines might learn how to create themselves and no longer require the proletariat as an intermediary. Although labour is the source of the atomist's profit, it is not the labour of humanity that is generating profit, but the labour of the automated machines produced by workers. In other words: the proletariat is losing its moral prerogative against the bourgeoisie the moment they lose their labour as a valuable commodity to the bourgeois class.

The proletariat have to wage a revolution in order to avoid the falling rates of their own labour as a valuable commodity and legitimate measurement of all created value. Marxism rests on human labour value. If human labour value is disvalued; then Marxism is disvalued as a legitimate revolutionary theory alongside it. Egoism rests on owning value; as long as you own something, even yourself, egoism shall endure as a legitimate revolutionary theory. The socialists have one last chance to wage their revolution before the atomists disvalue human labour.

The proletariat, once it has achieved the goals of communism, bears an uncanny resemblance to the serf of feudal society. The proletariat, transformed into the serf-proletariat, now has to give up the fruits of his labour to society at large; in turn this society accumulates that wealth and it becomes Communal Capital. This communal capital is used to repair and develop the means of production as well as to supply, and revitalise the labour powers of the serf-proletarian. The revitalization of the labour powers is, in other words, a communal pay rate amounting to the labourer's needs. It could be another word for a communal wage. The communist mode of production, like its predecessor, also has contradictions within itself.

As an example, the bourgeoisie cannot exist without constantly revolutionising the means of production, and thereby the relations of production, and with them the whole relations of society. On the other hand, the serf-proletarian of communism wants to preserve the old modes of production in unaltered form; it fears greatly the rise of a self-maintained means of production such as automatons able to labour by themselves with little to no assistance of the proletarian. The proletariat of socialism, however, gives rise to these automatons, to empower the means of production; to make them stronger in comparison to other existing capitalist societies. When communism is at long-last achieved, it takes on a feudal character. The serf-proletarian fears the further development of the means of production, in the same way the feudal nobility feared the further development of the means of production as it slowly caused the extinction of their class. The bourgeoisie of capitalism causes their own downfall through the revolutionising of the means of production because contradictions develop between the owner of the means of production, his property and the wage-slave proletarian. In stateless communism: the same thing happens, the owners of the means of production (serf-proletarians) start to develop a contradiction between themselves and the means of production itself. The communist mode of production is the last antagonistic form of the social process of production, but the productive forces developing within communist society also create the material conditions for a solution of this antagonism. The history of human society accordingly closes with this social formation.

Communism has agglomerate production concentrated in the hands of all, yet, communism is met by its antithetical contradiction in its mode of production. Since the communist mode of production has concentrated production into the hands of all people, it will cause the means of production to develop to such an extent where they can manage themselves via automatons and self-automated machinery; production will be placed in fewer and fewer hands; eventually in the hands of egoist individuals. The need and demand for serf-proletarians to manage the means of production will decrease to an all-time low through an epidemic of overproduction. We therefore find ourselves in the antithesis of communist production, the transformation of public production into individual production; this gives rise to the idlers as a class. Throughout the idler's struggle with the serf-proletarian, slowly we see the means of production being placed in fewer hands; until there comes a time when society no longer owns the means of production as a whole, but each individual owns his own means of production for his own egoistic self. The feudal nobility wanted to preserve the old means of production, since the further development of the means of production caused their extinction. The bourgeoisie wanted to revolutionise the means of production to birth themselves as a social class, but also found their doom through contradictions within the capitalist mode of production.

The serf-proletariat are the last historic phase of the proletariat as a social class. The serf-proletariat, like the serf under feudal nobility, wants to preserve the old means of production because further development implies the means of production being placed in fewer hands, causing the downfall of communism; and are not the workers of a communist society really semi-owner peasants? They own the means of production but at the same time, it is society at large that is the true owner over the means of production, and they fear greatly the further improvement in production which may cause the acceleration of their eventual extinction. They may own the land they work upon but every year they become short of about half the food they need and have to make up for this deficit by working on other pastures or selling more of their labour power to society, or even petty trading. The reason why they may be short on food at the end of the year is because of an influx of idlers that eat way too much without contributing anything at all. The idler wants to revolutionise the means of production; because through this he births himself into existence as a social class. The idler, through revolutionising the means of production, causes the downfall of the serf-proletarians as a meaningful class and because the idler depends on the serf-proletarians' labour for his sustenance, the idler class also meets its own downfall. This causes individuals to seize the means of production for themselves as their own property to serve their own interests for the sake of survival. Those that manage to do this become the first transformed egoists standing upon the ruins of communist society. The uncanny resemblance between the serf-proletarian and the serf under feudal nobility, or the bourgeoisie and the idler have never been so clear. Therefore, it is clear to the reader that this is a case of one of the dialectical materialist laws: The Negation of the Negation. The apparent return of the old in the new, wherein each stage of development overcomes its predecessor and incorporates its positive elements into a higher synthesis. A few pages into The Idler's Manifesto and we have already affirmed that the basis of the manifesto's assertions is in the three dialectical laws proposed by Friedrich Engels in his book, *Dialectics of Nature* which are as follows: 'The law of the transformation of quantity into quality and vice versa; The law of the interpenetration of opposites; The law of the negation of the negation' Through these laws of the dialectic, the idler and the worker enter into this class struggle which is the motor of their history and all that remains to be sorted out is the 'Victory or defeat - between the two alternatives the fate of the combat wavers. The victor becomes the lord, the vanquished the subject; the former exercises supremacy and "rights of supremacy," the later fulfils in awe and deference the "duties of the subject" but both remain enemies, and always lie in wait: they watch for each other's weaknesses.'

What do the idlers want, and what do the serf-proletarians want? The idlers want to live as parasites on the labour of others and the serf-proletariat wants everyone to be a worker and abolish idleness. Henceforth, class antagonism, which is often associated with a class society, rears its ugly head. One such antagonism is between idlers and workers, which will persist even in this "classless communist society" even though antagonism is usually associated with "class," this is certainly food for thought for our communists. They begin to understand that communism is not the last phase of history. The communist mode of production brings about antagonisms between idlers and workers, and their difference from each other and how they relate to production lend them enough credit for each to be called their own respective social class. The classless communist society, which for a long time we thought was perfect and utopian, is no longer classless, and if classes remerge, so does the organ of class rule - the state. Joseph Stalin in his *Economic Problems of the USSR* had incorrectly assumed that 'Undoubtedly, with the abolition of capitalism and the exploiting system in our country, and with the consolidation of the socialist system, the antagonism of interests between town and country, between industry and agriculture, was also bound to disappear. And that is what happened. The immense assistance rendered by the socialist town, by our working class, to our peasantry in eliminating the landlords and kulaks strengthened the foundation for the alliance between the working class and the peasantry, while the systematic supply of first-class tractors and other machines to the peasantry and its collective farms converted the alliance between the working class and the peasantry into friendship between them.' Here we notice how the technology of the tractor and machines actually aided the peasantry in being allied in a friendship with the industrial proletariat. That being said, while industrial technology aided the peasantry to develop a friendship with proletarians, automated technologies and artificial intelligence provide the direct opposite result as they continue to intensify these antagonisms between the workers and the idlers. Undoubtedly, with the birth of communism, the antagonism of interests between idlers and workers, between the megatropolis and the industrial towns is bound to reappear rather than disappear. Undoubtedly, only the abolition of communism and public property, with the consolidation of the egoist system, can the antagonisms of interest between the automated megatropolis and the industrial town be bound to disappear.

What is this idler class that we are speaking about? How do we define them? The idler is he who does no labour of his own, but survives through parasitically extracting the wealth of hard-working labourers. No society can evolve this parasitic class more than the communist society that has no protection against such parasites; for it no longer has a state machinery. With no state machinery to protect the interests of the labourers, communist society can only succumb to the idlers. The workers are the ones creating the surplus value, yet the idlers are the ones receiving the benefits. The idlers do not work, yet they are provided with the same level of luxuries as workers who contribute to the economy. This unfair distribution of resources can cause frustration and resentment among the working class; as the number of idlers continue to grow, there is likely to be a growing class tension within communist society.

In the last century, socialism has evolved upon capitalism's ability to create colossal productive forces. In a few years alone, the USSR, China and other socialist countries had become rightful equals in terms of productive forces and political economy when compared to America which was hundreds of years old; therefore, we have proof that socialism evolves productive forces at a much higher rate than found under capitalism. Henceforth, we can assume that the productive forces will be all the much stronger in communism when compared to the socialist stage. The subjection of nature's force to the labouring man would have been complete but the individual's subjection of nature's forces is merely at its beginning. We see then: the means of social production and of social exchange, whose foundation the dictatorship of the proletariat has built itself upon, were generated by capitalist society. At a certain stage in the development of the means of production and exchange, the conditions under which capitalist society produced and exchanged, its bourgeois relations of property were no longer compatible with the fast-developing productive forces owned by the workers in socialist states; therefore, these so-called organisations of capitalism within socialism were burst asunder. Through this bursting of the highest stage of capitalism, comes the ragamuffin-society of communism. The free competition of capitalism is replaced by sharing, as Max Stirner said, 'Against competition there rises up the principle of ragamuffin society - partition.' "Which is then accompanied by a social and political constitution that says, either integrate and become serf-proletarian or perish!" Partitioning is the communist ideal whereby, the society of serf-proletariat, after its labour is done, must give up the fruits of their labour, and in exchange, the whole of society takes a piecemeal out of the fruits of that labour done collectively; it is, in simplest terms, sharing wealth or giving goods for free amongst each other, which is the opposite principle of free competition found in capitalism. Although this "giving goods for free" principle, we soon discover, isn't actually free, but requires the toil of the labourer as an equal exchange.

Communist society cannot tolerate idlers, and yet, it is this society itself that creates such individuals who become idlers through the progression of automation and the communist mode of production. The process has already commenced due to the Automative Revolution that is on the horizon. The newly created idlers of the Automative Revolution are already struggling against the upper classes, such as with the Tangpingists, and the Bai Lan Movement in China. They do not struggle through unionisms or general strikes but they simply struggle by 'doing nothing' to further accelerate the abolition of labour. The Tangpingists and other idlers might temporarily unite with the proletariat in a struggle against the bourgeoisie.

At this stage, the idlers do not fight their enemies, but the enemies of their enemies; the remnants of the atomist bourgeoisie, national bourgeoisie and the industrial bourgeoisie; thus, the whole historical movement is concentrated in the hands of the proletariat: every victory so obtained is a victory for the proletariat.

The communists celebrate their October Revolution in the month of October, well the egoists also celebrate the month of October and declare it the spookiest month of the year, for which the spookiest events in history have happened. One example being the aforementioned October Revolution, which brought about a most nocturnal spookery into our world.

Modern communist society with its relations of production, of communal exchange and of public property, has conjured up self-maintaining and automated means of production and social exchange, that, like a coven of nocturnal sorcerers in the depths of a spooky All Hallow's Eve, have lost control of their collective powers over the thinnest veil between the living and the dead.

What leads to the birth of the idler class in communist society? We answer this question through the dialectical law of the passage of quantitative changes into qualitative changes that simply states that gradual and incremental changes can accumulate over time and eventually lead to a fundamental transformation in the nature of a system or phenomenon. For example, a gradual increase in temperature can eventually cause water to boil and transform from a liquid to a gas. If we apply the same law to communist society, we get the following conclusion: when communist society becomes so economically abundant with resources, the need for labourers and labour decreases. If the falling rates of profit presents a downfall of the bourgeoisie; then the falling rates of labour as a valuable commodity is the bane of the proletariat. When communist society has developed the means of production to become self-automated with minimal maintenance required from the serf-proletariat, this causes the demand and need of serf-proletarians to decrease. This is called the epidemic of overproduction. This quantitative change in the economics of a communist society leads to the qualitative changes of labourers being transformed into idlers. What has made the idler class possible is the elimination of the economy and the wage system as we know it.

In the lower phase of communism, the further development of the means of production causes a crisis: it starts to transform serf-proletarians into idlers causing the productive forces to be manned by fewer hands. This implies less wealth and abundance to restore the vitality of the labourers and poorer conditions of living; which leads to economic crashes where the serf-proletarians are not enough in number to man the impossibly large means of production that have developed over centuries. Since technology has evolved to such a state, that it can feed everyone with little to no labour, the dictatorship of the proletariat withers away and achieves a temporary high-end phase of communism, not knowing that what they have really achieved is a new economic crisis.

When production is high, abundance is also high. When abundance is high; the serf-proletarian dissociates himself from labour and becomes an idler. The influx of idlers leads to loss of labour, and henceforth, loss of abundance in goods; a loss of goods imply starvation, poverty. This will force some idlers to associate themselves with labour again, to be transformed temporarily back into serf-proletarians to fix the problem of poverty; that being said, some idlers who now find themselves comfortable in their idleness remain idle. Per each economic crisis cycle, the bulk of idlers comfortable in their idleness increases, causing the next economic crises to be worse and worse. As the number of idlers continues to increase, the production of basic needs also decreases in proportion, which means that basic needs are being consumed at a faster pace than can be produced, which would cause poverty whether one is an idler or a serf-proletarian. Such an economic crash in communist society would resemble, in some ways, capitalistic economic crashes, one could remember the Great Recession of 2008 or the Great Depression of the 1930's in the United States.

Automation, although it may help alleviate some of the major symptoms with an economic crisis in the short-term, becomes an even more problematic issue in the long-term because it causes a greater influx of idlers, thus shortening the demand for labour that has been automated. In other words, further automation only increases the length, time, and conditions of an economic crisis cycle due to shortage of certain labour in some industries.

Therefore, this is the ironic contradiction; the productive forces are the most colossal they have ever been but the people that man and utilise the means of production are at an all-time low. The serf-proletarians attempt to rectify that problem by building even more powerful productive forces – to sustain all the populations with an abundance of needs and resources. All this further development of machinery is a short-term solution to the problem of the communist mode of production; in actual fact, this short-term solution keeps on adding to the problems of this mode of production. The further development of the means of production for a temporary period of time would manage to restore the original abundance of wealth and needs at society's disposal, but over time, the automatons – the means of production themselves, would have replaced most of the essential parts of human labour; therefore, causing the further extinction of the workers. It is therefore clear that in these crises, the previous means of production are periodically destroyed to create new, more developed productive forces. Henceforth, as the serf-proletariat starts to develop his consciousness as a social class; he starts to recognize that the further development of the means of production will cause even more poverty and scattering among the masses. He starts to cut down on the development of productive forces, and even starts to preserve the means of production, as they currently are in order to preserve their existence and relevance as a social class; the serf-proletariat would start to protest the development of artificial intelligence and automation that places their class into danger.

Communist society, having developed productive forces to such a tremendous extent, becomes enmeshed in contradictions which it is unable to solve. By producing large and larger quantities of commodities, and reducing their price to zero according to the needs of the masses, communism intensifies partitioning, ruins the mass of serf-proletarians and converts them into idlers. On the other hand, by expanding production and concentrating the hands of billions of workers in huge factories, communism lends the process of production a communal and social character, which thus undermines its own foundation, in as much as the individual act of appropriation demands the individual and egoist ownership of the means of production. Yet the means of production remain public communist property, which is incompatible with the individual and egoist appropriation of one's needs. Henceforth, because the character of production is a social act, but the character of appropriating needs for oneself is the most individualistic act, there is inherently an incompatibility in the mode of production. On one hand, production is a collective process, while acquiring needs for myself is entirely my individual act and freedom; the communist mode of production divides the collectivists against the individualists. As Max Stirner said, 'In general, all states, constitutions, churches, have sunk by the secession of individuals; for the individual is the irreconcilable enemy of every generality' Henceforth, the individual becomes the ultimate irreconcilable contradiction against communist society, empowered by its contradictions in the mode of production. While production is a social act, exchange and appropriation continue to be individual acts, the acts of individuals. In other words, as a serf-proletarian, I labour and produce the wealth of society alongside others, but when it comes time to appropriate or receive my fair end of the bargain in the form of an exchange, this is entirely up to me as an individual whether I want to take my fair share of my labour in goods, or whether I want to far exceed the share of my labour as goods. The anarchy of appropriation is born within the mode of production. There is still an anarchy of production in communism, because although it might to some extent be a planned economy, there is no way for the serf-proletarians to limit what the people can appropriate without abandoning the principle of free appropriation and thus abandoning communism. What I have appropriated today might not be what I appropriate tomorrow, the needs of individuals are volatile. Therefore, communist society must always be geared towards producing superabundance and overproduction in order that everyone may be fed.

These irreconcilable contradictions between the character of the productive forces and the relations of production makes themselves felt more in the periodical crisis of overproduction. When communists find no effective demand for their goods, owing to the ruin of the mass of the population which they themselves have brought about, they are compelled to burn products, destroy manufactured goods, suspend production, and destroy productive forces at a time when millions of people are forced towards unemployment. Henceforth, the idler class is born not because there are not enough goods circulating in the economy, but only because there is an overproduction of goods circulating. This implies that the communist relations of production have ceased to correspond to the state of productive forces of society and have come into irreconcilable contradiction with them.

In communist society, everything is reversed. It is no longer the ruling class that exploits, but the subordinate class that does the exploiting; in other words, the subordinate idler exploits the dominant serf-proletarian, but the proletarian is still the ruling ideology and class. Since the idler reintroduces exploitation, he is paving the way towards overcoming the serf-proletariat as the ruling dominant class; the idler plans to become the ruling class over the serf-proletariat as a subordinate class under idler rule. The idlers have to seize the means of production and organise the people who are involved in the process of production, thus becoming the ruling class.

Communism is pregnant with revolution, whose mission it is to replace the existing communist ownership of property by egoist ownership.

Communist society starts to find itself in the same sad condition of capitalist society – the absurdity of the epidemic of overproduction. When communist society finds itself in a state of famine, barbarism, idlers extracting wealth from proletarians; where it seems as if someone had cut off the supply line of subsistence itself: the communists will find themselves in perpetual poverty. Why does this happen? It is because in communism too, there is too much civilization, too much industry, commerce, subsistence. The productive forces at society's disposal no longer tend to the development of the conditions of communal property; on the contrary, they have become too powerful, even for all of the men in society by which they are fettered; thus, bringing disorder into communist society and endangering the existence of the public ownership of public property.

How do the serf-proletarians get over these crises? On one hand by continuing to develop the productive forces to make up for the constant loss of workers, which is one of the prime causes of these crises in the first place. On the other hand, through the conquest of society, by re-establishing laws, regulations, government, the regression to the dictatorship of the proletariat, to rebuild a state machinery in order to force these idlers back into the labouring force, and therefore reverting gradually to socialism – further destabilising communism. That is to say, the serf-proletariat get over these economic crises by short-term solutions that seem to work in the immediate present but have even more catastrophic and destructive effect in the long-term, paving the way for even worse economic crises rather than diminishing the means whereby crises are produced. The unity of internationalism, the populations from all corners of the world that communism has established starts to wither into disunity, fracturing, the reestablishment of borders and nations; as well as scattering the populations into rural cities and transforming them once more into feudal-like barbarians.

The weapons with which the communist industrial proletariat felled capitalism to the ground are now turned against the proletariat themselves. Not only have the proletariat forged the weapons that bring about their own death; they have also called into existence the men who are to wield those weapons – the modern class of paupers – The Idlers.

The communists were quite content to use dialectical materialism in order to demolish capitalism and dialectically put-up communism. Do you communists actually have an inkling that you have been beaten with your own weapons? What retort can you hearty fellows make against it, when I again dialectically demolish what you have just dialectical put up? You have shown me with what eloquence one can transform private property into public property, capitalism into communism. What do you have against it, when I turn your neat trick back on you? When, through dialectical materialism, I demolish communism and dialectically put-up egoism? Nothing but an inkling! Therefore, let me give you hearty fellows an inkling of your own medicine as a dish best served cold.

Let us continue to decorate this dish with layers of analysis. In proportion, 'as the bourgeoisie, i.e. capital, is developed, in the same proportion is the proletariat, the modern working class, developed - a class of labourers, who live only as long as they find work, and who only find work only so long as their labour increases capital' says Karl Marx in the *Communist Manifesto*. But let us say, as is frequently happening in the 21th century, that the working class's labour no longer increases capital because an automation can increase capital triplefold, what happens to the working class then? Marx would then have to agree using his own logic that the lower strata of the middle class - the petit bourgeoisie, the labour aristocrats, the industrial bourgeoisie, and the industrial proletariat - all these sink gradually into the pauper; partly because their diminutive capital does not suffice for the scale on which modern industry is carried on, and is swamped in the competition with the large atomist capitalists; and partly because their specialised skills is rendered worthless by the new methods of production that mainly involve digitization, artificial intelligence, and automation. Thus, the idler, or the pauper, is recruited from all classes of the population. The industrial proletariat, finding themselves in danger of extinction at this point, organise one last attempt at a proletarian revolution as they recite images, songs, anthems of past struggles, uniting under the banner of Marx, Engels, Lenin, Stalin, and Mao once again. As Marx made clear when reciting Hegel, 'all great world-historic facts and personages appear, so to speak, twice … the first time as tragedy, the second time as farce' and as we can see, the modernised Marxism-Leninism-Maoism of the Atomist Age is nothing but political bankruptcy of the highest order, a mere satire of the original proletarian struggle of centuries ago, a farce and a comedy.

The idlers at this point would already exist - the fact that this manifesto is being penned is proof that they already exist in the minority. While the idlers are still a minority, they may not yet understand their true struggle, they may aid the proletariat against the atomist bourgeoisie and put an end to capitalism once and for all. The real struggle of the vagabond's revolution comes after the proletarian attempts at revolution whether successful or unsuccessful. If the proletarian revolution is a success; then it merely means that the idler's antagonistic relationship with the burgeoning serf-proletariat can be better illustrated and pronounced. Once this occurs the reunited banners of Marx, Engels, Lenin, Stalin, Mao and even Gonzalo will belong in the dustbin of history.

The idler goes through various stages of development: at first, it struggles against the atomist bourgeoisie; then it struggles against its main enemy: the serf-proletarian. At first the contest is carried on by individual idlers, then by the idle workers within the factories, then by the operatives of the trades of mental labour, in one locality, against the individual serf-proletarians who now exploit them though the renewed dictatorship of the proletariat. The idlers direct their attacks not against the serf-proletarians' conditions of production, but against the instruments of production themselves: they destroy imported wares that compete with their idleness, they smash machinery to pieces, they set factories ablaze, they seek to restore, by force, the vanished status of the idler from the late-stage communist phase. In this late phase, the workers sell themselves, piecemeal, as a commodity to society at large, like any article of commerce; and in exchange, they get back according to their needs. The worker is consequently exposed to all the vicissitudes of partitioning, to all the fluctuations that come with the principles: "From each according to their abilities; to each according to their needs." Yet, division of needs is also partitioning; and division of labour is a contradiction in and off itself that's set to blow like a time bomb.

Communal capital is developed side by side with the modern working class of communism, who survive so long as their labour increases communal capital. We find that the more communal capital increases to supply the needs for the labourers, the more the working day decreases hour by hour until it results in some serf-proletarians working less hours than in other sectors of industry, and some being out of labour, idle for months and years. These serf-proletarians must sell themselves as a communal commodity, and like every article of commerce, are exposed to partitioning: to all the fluctuations of communist society. The labourer loses all individual character as a workman and becomes not only an appendage of the machine, but a mere addendum to the automaton machine, causing so much division of labour that labour cannot be divided any further and becomes almost indivisible. His labour becomes the monotonous activity of providing maintenance to the means of production themselves, to maintain the means of production. The productive forces, and communist society as a whole, become one clogged cogwheel of industrial machinery, an intricate organism that has metal and machines at every turn: a means of production that has evolved past the need of requiring a human labourer. The division of labour transforms into the gradual abolishment of labour itself as the automaton or the machine replaces most aspects of human labour. Labour is divided like the atom until it can no longer be divided - the point of no return; when labour can no longer be divided, it is safe to say that 'labour has been abolished.' The use of machinery and division of labour continue to increase, as man's job becomes only the maintenance of colossal productive forces, the billions of parts of machinery. In proportion therefore, 'as the repulsiveness of the work increases,' the social needs which are given to each individual are decreased. Thus, poverty would become the norm.

The famous anarchist Kropotkin also noted this problem of the epidemic of overproduction in his dreamy vision of a communist utopia as he stated, 'Who will have a right to the food of the commune? will assuredly be the first question which we shall have to ask ourselves. Every township will answer for itself, and we are convinced that the answers will all be dictated by the sentiment of justice. Until labour is reorganised, as long as the disturbed period lasts, and while it is impossible to distinguish between inveterate idlers and genuine workers thrown out of work, the available food ought to be shared by all without exception.' Even Kropotkin felt deep within himself that there are contradictions between idlers and workers. Problems would arise when food provisions run short as a result of too many idlers and not enough workers. Kropotkin attempts to brush the idler problem aside by stating "provisions will run short in a month!" "So much the better," say we; "it will prove that, for the first time on record, the people have had enough to eat." Without a doubt, we can answer Kropotkin's statements about provision shortages being a result of the same epidemic of production present in capitalism. Kropotkin states that 'A society where work is free will have nothing to fear from idlers' but of course, the fact that throughout his book, he mentions the idler, idleness and laziness oddly much, signifies his fear for this new enemy of the proletariat; in addition, if labour is free, it has no value for me to engage in. But surely you are an artist, a writer, or a sculptor?

Surely profit and value are not your only motivations to work? Yes, I find art and writing interesting; alas these things do not feed the population. If labour has lost its intrinsic value; then I no longer see a value in prolonging it. Thus, it runs, as Max Stirner once said, that 'If labour becomes free, the state is lost.' And for Stirner, communism was yet another state because society becomes master over the means of production; thus, labour is not really free. Stirner states this himself when he says, 'On the contrary, communism, by the abolition of all personal property, only presses me back still more into dependence on another, namely, on the generality or collectively; and, loudly as it always attacks the 'state,' what it intends is itself again a state.' Therefore, the conclusion is this, When Stirner was talking about the state being lost because labour is free, he was not talking about communism but rather egoism. Stirner, in conclusion, argues that communism, through its own inherent contradictions, would bring about the devaluing of labour, to the point where labour is considered worthless. He called this worthlessness the pauperism of the state. Communism is the highest development of the state but it is also the last state in history. Communism, through its own cheapening of labour, shall abolish labour itself and the masses, then labour truly becomes 'free,' because its entire value has become equivalent to nothing. Because now labour produces nothing - it is only capable of producing idlers who enter into political existence; These idlers then experience an overall struggle against the serf-proletarians, which is merely Stirner's creative nothing asserting itself over the dialectical materialism of the communists. The union of egoists that is formed on the ruins of communist society is merely the end result of the idlers' class war against the workers. The conclusion of this struggle would lead the idlers to transform themselves from worthless paupers, into the egoist owner, [Eigner] in other words, they would have managed from relative obscurity, worthlessness and nothing, to create something from nothing. This is the creative nothing. This something new is the union of egoists which replaces communist society that is now in ruin. Communism therefore leads us to egoism; not the other way round as Engels once tried to argue.

If the noble feudal prince Kropotkin were to become a manager of his dream commune, he would soon find that the idlers are becoming way too much of a problem - the only way to solve the idler problem is to unite with other workers to manage these idlers and forcibly take control of their lives in such a way that they must rejoin the working force. Idlers would at first delight in their laziness, taking the fill of their needs but providing no labour in exchange. Over time, the labourers have to accelerate the expansion of automation to compensate for this loss of labour; yet, this takes time to implement, and society would experience the depletion of provisions within a month. Thus, pauperism and poverty would be the order of the day.

Modern industry would have to cope by converting the large factories with thousands of workers into smaller workshops operating highly efficient robotics. The masses of labourers are no longer crowded in factories organised like soldiers, but instead, are taken out of the factory and placed into crowded and diseased streets. Each of these paupers is disorganised, lifeless and isolated from each other - thus begins the decay of the organised masses and the greatest crisis of poverty known to mankind. This poverty is not only a material poverty but also the poverty of each individual in his character.

The serf-proletariat can see this point of no return dawning on the horizon, and in order to save labour from being thoroughly abolished; they blame the idler class that is becoming more numerous. They blame the laziness of this new class for their ills rather than the means of production which brought about their existence. Therefore, in a last-ditch attempt to resolve the problems of communist society and to restore its beautiful splendour, that utopian dream and vision, the workers unite as they have always done against parasites in order to squash the idlers. They unite into a government; they restore the dictatorship of the proletariat that is the only thing that is capable of keeping the idler in check. They start to construct new state machinery in order to put a stop to this exploitation, and in a way, they manage to succeed. They have now succeeded in cutting away the source of the idler's parasitic livelihood, leaving him little choice but to join the labouring force again, transforming himself once more into a serf-proletarian. At what cost do they manage to succeed? By regression into socialism, the further destabilisation of communism as a society, and by furthermore highlighting the internal contradictions between idlers and serf-proletarians. Henceforth, their so-called victory against the idler is really a loss, as it is through their own actions that communist society is further destabilised, damaged to the point of no repair. At this point, communist society is no longer stateless, the workers have seen to that, it is also no longer classless because as we have shown, there is an ongoing class struggle between idlers and workers; finally, communism is no longer moneyless because the state, in order to manage the idlers, would have to reintroduce the concept of money in an attempt to control and track appropriation. We are therefore reintroduced to the Trilemma of Communist Society. If communism births new classes into existence, then it follows that an organ of class rule or a state must also be born alongside the ruling class that subjugates the lesser class. In fewer words: if communism has social classes; then it must have a state, and vice versa. If classes and states exist; then there must be money at the core to subjugate one class or another. Henceforth if communism is no longer stateless, no longer classless, no longer moneyless; then it is no longer a communist society but rather a regressed socialist society.

At this stage, the idlers still form an incoherent mass scattered all over different localities across the world, broken up by their mutual partitioning. If anywhere they unite to form more compact bodies, this is not yet the consequence of their own active union of egoists, but of the union of the proletarians, which, in order to attain its own political ends, is compelled to set the whole lumpen in motion and for a time is able to do so.

The bulk of these idlers revert back into serf-proletarians; the few idlers that remain are the most revolutionary of the lot, these few become the revolutionary ground upon which the Idler's Revolution is built.

With the development of industry, the idler not only increases in number; but becomes concentrated in greater masses, its strength grows, and it feels that strength more. The various interests and conditions of life within the ranks of the idler are more and more equalised, in proportion to the advancement of automation; automated industry, alongside the renewed dictatorship of the proletariat, obliterates all distinctions of labour, nearly everywhere reducing social wages to the same low level. The growing partitioning among the serf-proletarians lead to further commercial crises, and fluctuating the social wage of labour even further. Now that the serf-proletarians find themselves no longer threatened by the idler, they feel free to improve the machinery; The unceasing improvement of machinery, ever more rapidly developing, makes the livelihood of the idler more and more precarious; the collisions between individual idlers and individual serf-proletarians take more the character of collisions between two classes. Thereupon, the idlers begin to form combinations (unions of egoists) against the serf-proletariat; they club together in order to keep up the rate of social wages or needs; they form temporary associations in order to make provisions for these occasional revolts, which then take shape into several riots. Henceforth, a conscious revolutionary mass movement of idlers must form into several unions and associations. The towering genius and sharpest intellect that is Dr. Samuel Johnson once said, 'If you are idle, be not solitary. If you are solitary, do not be idle' therefore, let the idlers of the world never be solitary again and voluntarily unite in a common purpose. The unity of the proletariat can be shaken only by the unity of the idler!

The whole aim of these unions is to eventually restore the conditions of communism; upon which the idler is free to extract as much surplus value from society without any impositions or limit. At first, they are content with merely an increase of the wages provided by this new renewed dictatorship controlled by the serf-proletarians. The idlers are victorious every now and then; the real battle lies not in the immediate result, however, but in the ever-expanding union of the egoists. This union is helped on by the improved automated means of guerilla warfare and communication created by modern industry which help the idlers get in contact with one another. It is this contact with each other that is needed to centralise the numerous struggles between classes.

This organisation of the idlers into a class, and consequently into a political union or party, is continually being upset by the partitioning of the idlers themselves, yet, every time, it rises up again; stronger, firmer, mightier. It compels, at first, legislative recognition of particular interests of the idlers, by taking advantage of the divisions among the serf-proletarians itself: thus, the universal basic income that is being attempted today will be carried once more in the future.

Collision between the classes of the old society, in many ways, is what directs the course of development for the idlers. The serf-proletariat would find itself involved in a constant battle, at first with the industrial bourgeoisie and the atomist bourgeoisie. Later on, with those portions of the serf-proletarians itself, whose interests have become antagonistic to the progress of industry; such as the industrial proletariat who find themselves altogether antagonistic to the atomisation of industry which breaks down industry, as if it were an atom in fission, causing a nuclear reaction that brings about the industrial proletarian's extinction. The proletariat itself, therefore, supplies the idlers with its own instruments of political and general education, in other words, it furnishes the idlers with weapons for fighting the proletariat.

Entire sections of the ruling classes become, by the advance of industry, precipitated into the idlers, or are at least threatened in their conditions of existence; all the while, supplying the idlers with fresh elements of enlightenment and progress. Finally, when class struggle nears the decisive hour, this process of dissolution occurring within the serf-proletarian ruling class assumes a violent character. A small section of the ruling class cuts itself adrift, and joins the revolutionary class of idlers that hold the future in their hands. In the same manner that, in the past, a section of the bourgeoisie went over to the proletariat; now a portion of the serf-proletarians goes over to the idlers and in particular, a portion of serf-proletarian ideologists, whom had raised themselves to the level of comprehending theoretically the historical movement as a whole.

Of all the classes that stand face to face with the workers, the idler alone is a really revolutionary class. The other classes decay and finally disappear in the face of modern industry; the idler is its own special and essential product. The atomist bourgeoisie, the industrial bourgeoisie, the petit bourgeoisie, the old industrial proletariat; all these fight against the idlers to save themselves from extinction as fractions of the middle class. They are therefore not revolutionary, but conservative and reactionary; for they wish to roll back the wheel of history. If by any chance they are revolutionary, they are so only in the view of their impending transfer into the idler class. The non-dangerous classes, the paper tiger classes, the social scum, that passively rotting mass thrown off the lowest layers of old industrial society, may, here and there, be swept into the movement by an idler's revolution; its conditions of life, however, prepare it far more for the part of a bribed tool of reactionary intrigue.

Communists may find this confusing: how has the idler, the undesirable class of history, now become a revolutionary class and the proletariat have become a reactionary class? Why have the tables turned? Through the application of dialectical materialism, which the communists have given to the idlers to use against them, we will find our answer. The conditions of the idlers, those of old society at large, are virtually swamped. The idlers are propertyless; therefore, private or public property, law, family, national character, religion, work, they are all prejudices of the old society - in other words, spooks.

The materialistic conditions of communism are ripe for the development of the idler class. A communist society that is stateless, classless, moneyless, with labourers producing wealth free for the taking, leaves the idler free to produce no labour and exploit the labour value of others. The more it becomes aware of itself as a class, the more it will act as a social class. From the weakest of all social classes, it shall become the mightiest of all social classes, that has qualities from all the other social classes and none of their weaknesses. From the weakest vagabond class of the capitalist epoch shall rise the strongest of them all. The idler rises to become just that. On the other hand, the proletarian class, from a position of power, descends gradually into a position of weakness, sharing elements of the feudal serf, and the depressed industrial proletariat.

All the preceding classes that got the upper hand sought to fortify their already acquired status by subjecting society at large to their conditions of appropriation. The idlers cannot become masters of the productive forces of society, except by abolishing their own previous communist mode of appropriation, and thereby also every other previous mode of appropriation. They have nothing of their own to secure or fortify, their mission is to destroy all precious securities for, and insurances of, public property. The idler's movement is the self-conscious, independent movement of the immense majority, in the interests of the immense majority. All previous historical movements were movements of the minority with the exception of the industrial proletariat, which, from a majority, is falling down to a minority. The idlers are the direct result of the proletariat's fall from grace. The idlers shall eventually find themselves in the class of the highest majority in history - the further revolutionising of the means of production does not threaten their existence like it does the workers, but continues to enhance them.

Marx too, agrees wholeheartedly with us when he states 'The modern labourer, on the contrary, instead of rising with the progress of industry, sinks deeper and deeper below the conditions of existence of his own class. He becomes a pauper, and pauperism develops more rapidly than population and wealth.' The industrial worker will become an "obsolete tool," much like the handicraftsman of old. Therefore, if you are a modern Marxist reading this text; then be a good Marxist and accept our manifesto's position rather than combat vehemently against it. Of course, modern Maoists might declare, in objection, that Marx was not a prophet and we should oppose book worship, to which they would be right. Mao Zedong once said, 'Whatever is written in a book is right — such is still the mentality of culturally backward Chinese peasants.' Strangely enough, within the same Communist Party there are also people who always, in discussion, say "Show me where it's written in the book!" Of course, we are not quoting Marx on pauperism because Marx is always right, but rather 'We need Marxism in our struggle,' because Marxism leads us to pauperism and the pauper leads us to Stirner's egoism. 'Of course, we should study Marxist books, but this study must be integrated with our country's actual conditions.' and this is exactly what this manifesto does, it overcomes book worship by 'investigating the actual situation.' We study the current conditions of the world through a Marxist perspective that has taken us beyond Marxism itself. Marxism has found itself transformed into egoism, as Stirner had predicted almost two centuries ago. The idea that communism would eventually lead to egoism. Who decides what is right? Those who have might decide what is right; not those who write. All the theorists in the world - Marx, Lenin, Mao and even Stirner would not be capable of any might if all they did was write. Book worship in Stirnerian circles is the mentality of culturally spooked egoists.

The idler, who is the lowest stratum of communist society, cannot raise itself up without the whole of official society being sprung up in the air. The serf in the period of serfdom raised himself to membership in the commune; just as the petty bourgeois, under the yoke of feudal absolutism, raised himself into the bourgeoisie. The industrial proletariat, under the yoke of the bourgeoisie, raised himself into the serf-proletariat of communism, master of the means of production. Yet, the modern serf-proletariat, on the contrary, instead of rising with the progress of industry, sinks deeper and deeper below his class's conditions of existence. He becomes an idling pauper, and pauperism develops more rapidly than anything else.

Here is therefore the evidence, that the serf-proletarian is no longer fit to be the ruling class in society, or to impose its conditions of existence upon society as an overriding law.: it is unfit to rule because it is incompetent to assure an existence to itself within the coming crisis of automation, because it cannot help letting itself sink into such a state, it has to feed the idler, instead of being fed by him. Society would no longer be able to live under these serf-proletarians, in other words, its existence is no longer compatible with society.

The essential condition for the existence, and for the sway of the serf-proletarian class, is the formation and augmentation of communal capital: the condition for this communal capital is communal wage-labour. Wage-labour rests exclusively on partitioning between the labourers. The advance of industry, whose involuntary promoter is the serf-proletarian, replaces the isolation of the idlers; due to partitioning or burden-sharing by their revolutionary combination, due to association. The development of modern industry, therefore, cuts from under its feet the very foundation on which the serf-proletariat produces and appropriates products. What the serf-proletarian therefore produces above all, is its own grave-diggers. Its fall and the victory of the idler are equally inevitable.

The only way for the serf-proletarian to survive is to create another state appendage to protect their interest, but this restoration of socialism would cause the downfall of communism.

Therefore, it is not at all surprising for communist society to regress back into the template of socialism. Even if the serf-proletarians do not regress back to the dictatorship of the proletariat, which is highly unlikely, the idlers would still wage a revolution against any person that prevents them from extracting the wealth of society, since this would be considered a form of state or government that regulates their freedom.

All property relations of the past have continually been subject to historical change consequent upon the change in historical conditions. The serf-proletariat, being transformed daily into the idler, henceforth becomes a weakened class of the few, and the idlers become the many. At first, it is the idlers that exploit surplus value to survive; when the serf-proletarians rebuild the state machinery of socialism, it is they that exploit surplus-value from the rest of the workers through the regression of public property into state property. The French revolution abolished feudal property in favour of bourgeois property; the Bolshevik revolution abolished private property in favour of state property; the communist revolution of the future shall abolish state property in favour of public property. The distinguishing feature of egoism is not the abolition of property generally, but the abolition of public property. Communism is the final, and most complete expression of a system of production and appropriation that is based on class antagonisms; on the exploitation of the few by the many. The idlers become so numerous that even the renewed dictatorship of the proletariat cannot contend with the idler's coming revolution. Henceforth, the idler (the many) exploits the few, the serf-proletarians. In communism we find the dialectical and antithetical opposite of exploitation in capitalism.; not the exploitation of the many by the few, but the exploitation of the few serf-proletarians by the many varied idlers.

In this sense, the theory of egoism may be summed up in the single sentence: Abolition of public property. Communism is public property per excellence; therefore, egoism can be said to be the next phase of history which intends to abolish the principle of public property, and free equal partitioning for the well-being of the individual. You are horrified at our intention to do away with public property; but in an existing communist society, public property is already done away with for tenths of the population; its existence for everyone is solely due to its non-existence in the hands of no particular individual. While in capitalism, only one-tenths or less could be said to hold property in their hands - in communism, no one owns property - everyone merely shares a piece from it while not owning any part of it; therefore, property under communism is given a ghostly and ethereal quality where it could be said to both exist and not exist at the same time: property is transformed into an even higher spook. The communists confuse this as property being abolished once and for all, but it has been merely given a phantasmic quality. Everyone shares it but no one owns it, so, it is not property that has been done away with, but the ownership of it.

Therefore, it could be said that ownership in communism does not exist. You reproach us, therefore, with the intent to do away with that form of public property, the necessary condition for whose existence, is the absence of any property for all individuals pertaining to that society. In other words, you reproach us with intending to do away with this ghostly property that is owned by no one, but rather, owned by a society. Far from Marxism, being an exact materialistic science - it is a most idealistic and imprecise science that plans for property to become an immaterial and ghostly concept. Egoism remedies this problem by stating 'Property, therefore, should not and cannot be abolished; it must rather be torn from ghostly hands and become my property.' Once again, property is owned by those mighty enough to claim it for themselves.

Public property, as a thesis, is posited against the free appropriation of goods as antithesis. Free appropriation of goods and public property annihilate one another and form in its place, my personal property, out of which I freely appropriate the property of others through my might.

But does labour create any property for the labourer in communism? Not a bit. It creates communal capital, i.e., that kind of ghostly property which exploits communal wage-labour, and which cannot increase, except upon condition of begetting a new supply of wage-labour for fresh exploitation. Property, in its ghostly form, is based on the antagonism of communal capital and communal wage labour. Let us examine both sides of this antagonism.

Communal 'Capital is a collective product, and only by the united action of many members, nay, in the last resort, only by the united action of all members of society, can it be set in motion. Capital is therefore not only personal; it is a social power. When, therefore, capital is converted into common property, into the property of all members of society, personal property is not thereby transformed into social property. It is only the social character of the property that is changed. It loses its class character.' Of course, while personal property remains personal property, private property becomes social property.

Let us now investigate communal wage-labour. In capitalism, wage-labour is the 'minimum wage,' i.e., that quantum of the means of subsistence which is absolutely requisite to keep the labourer in bare existence as a labourer' and communism does not 'intend to abolish this personal appropriation of the products of labour, an appropriation that is made for the maintenance and reproduction of human life, and that leaves no surplus wherewith to command the labour of others.' All that the communists want is to do away with the 'miserable character of this appropriation, under which the labourer lives merely to increase capital, and is allowed to live only insofar as the interest of the ruling class requires it' However, what the communists have not understood very well is that, under communism, this miserable character of appropriation under which the worker lives to increase capital still exists, because the worker, rather than increase the capital of the bourgeoisie, now increases the capital of society at large and is only allowed to live only insofar as he serves the interests of the ruling class - the workers. An idler, as an example, does not serve the interests of the workers. It is said that in 'bourgeois society, living labour is but a means to increase accumulated labour. In communist society, accumulated labour is but a means to widen, to enrich, to promote the existence of the labourer' but not to promote or enrich the existence of the idler who runs over and against the labourer. 'In bourgeois society, therefore, the past dominates the present; in communist society, the present dominates the past' but in the union of egoists, the present dominates the future. In communist society, wage-labour still exists, only this time, it serves to increase communal capital rather than the personal capital of the bourgeoisie. Whoever has the most capital is the ruling class of that society. In capitalism, the bourgeoisie have the most capital, in communism, it is the workers who have the most capital, and they are thus the ruling class. The idlers, despite not being the ruling class of this society, are the exploitative class who extract surplus value from the communal capital generated by the workers, and thus, they profit off this arrangement. This implies that the workers will not be the ruling class of this society for a very long time as their days are numbered. Egoism then has its task to fulfil: To change all social property and the social character of property into personal property with a personal character in regards to property. Everything becomes personal. Property becomes personal, capital ceases to be a social power and becomes only a personal power, classes and wage-labour of any kind cease to exist. While in capitalism, capital was both social and personal, the mode of production was socialised but the mode of appropriation was capitalistic, individualist and personal. In communism, capital is only a social power, the mode of production socialised; but appropriation remains an individual affair, thus even in this society there are antagonisms. Only egoism, therefore, that has personalised everything, has no contradictions or antagonisms. Thus, there are no longer any antagonisms between property, labour and capital, as all these things have become personal rather than impersonal.

Collective ownership of the means of production is not really ownership, but sharing; after all, I own my body, I do not share my body; if I shared my body in between two, or millions of consciousnesses, then I could not be said to own my body, only share it with others. This is what we mean by public ownership not being ownership at all, but rather an impersonal form of partitioning - sharing. The communists have no clue regarding a theory of ownership, neither do they know the true definition and meaning of the word. A factory or a piece of machinery which everybody owns, could also be said to be owned by nobody, like that famous proverb, 'A friend to everyone is a friend to no one,' likewise, 'A property for all is a property for none.' This is the doctrine of pauperism - of communism, but for the union of egoists, 'A property for me, and only me, is a property for all.'

The modern egoists have, as of late, taken an interest in the idea of Stirnerian Economics. Stirner himself had foreknowledge of economic theories, especially due to his translation of Adam Smith's *Wealth of Nations*. This is not to say that all of Stirner's knowledge of economics was based on theories associated with the bourgeoisie, we know that he formulated his own theory of value as he had also preconceived notions of the theories of value by Proudhon, the early communists, and even the young Marx. Max Stirner has his own economic theory and his own theory of value which he achieves through dialectical play between the theory of labour and the theory of idleness as forms of value. It would seem, at first glance, that Max Stirner is nihilistic when it comes to his own theory of value, but, after some investigation, it is clear that there is but one theory of value for Stirner. He makes clear when he says 'But my property is not a thing, since this has an existence independent of me; only my might is my own. Not this tree, but my might or control over it, is what is mine.' It becomes immediately clear that for Stirner, private property and public property are merely spooks. They are spooks because it's phantasmic to believe that such a thing as property can belong to someone, or that there's an intrinsic value which could buy private property with money.

For Stirner, this is the false principle of private property. In actual fact, private property is perpetrated through the grace of the state by allowing one to build private property in a given area, and maintained through authoritarian might. Henceforth, what people really own is not private or public property but rather their own ability to own things, to use their power to enforce the protection of that property. More property simply means more power, might to oneself. The public property of a communist society would be maintained and protected by the grace of its labourers, and its hidden subtle state machinery, as the communists loudly proclaim the state does not exist. For Stirner, property is not a physical thing, since this would somehow claim that it has an existence that is independent of me. If property had existence independent of me, it would also imply that there was some value to that property which is independent of me as an egoist.

Stirner comes to the conclusion that Ownness; not labour or capital, is the correct theory of value. The bourgeoisie might say, 'my capital gives value to property through profit,' and the communist ragamuffin will say, 'it's my labour that gives the value to the bourgeoisie in terms of profit,' but the egoist says: 'You fools! You have to own your labour to give value to the bourgeoisie, and the bourgeoisie has to own their capital in order to generate profit.' If one does not own oneself, does not own his labour or capital; then labour and capital by themselves cannot construct property, neither profit. The idler in communist society exists in order to subvert the labourer's theory of value, we referred to this earlier as the idler theory of value; that in communist society, labour starts to lose its value and, gradually, idleness becomes more valuable to the individual than labour. When the labourer's surplus theory of value clashes in contradiction against the idler's theory of value, both annihilate each other in the dialectic. Labour becomes valueless and idleness also becomes valueless: It leaves only the ability to own. Henceforth, Ownness, the ability to own whatever it is you like through your own power and might, becomes the only revealed theory of value; when this happens, we know the Idler's Revolution has been a success in bringing about the union of egoists.

Karl Marx, in his famous *Communist Manifesto*, is remembered to have said that 'Communism deprives no man of the power to appropriate the products of society; all that it does is to deprive him of the power to subjugate the labour of others by means of such appropriations. It has been objected that upon the abolition of private property, all work will cease, and universal laziness will overtake us. According to this, bourgeois society ought long ago to have gone to the dogs through sheer idleness; for those of its members who work, acquire nothing, and those who acquire anything do not work. The whole of this objection is but another expression of the tautology: that there can no longer be any wage-labour when there is no longer any capital.'

Communism deprives no man of the power to appropriate the products of society, this supposedly allows me to be free to appropriate all the products produced society as an egoist, in the same breath, Marx says that communist society deprives the individual from the power to subjugate the labour of others by means of such appropriations. Henceforth, I am free to appropriate products from society, but the communist mode of production deprives me from the power to subjugate the labour of others through the extraction of surplus value. How then, does communist society have the authority to deprive me of the power as an idler to subjugate the surplus value of others? If it is supposed to be a classless society, then by what power does communism deprive me of power to subjugate the labourer's surplus value? This is a question only the great Marx can answer. But first, while it may be true that conservatives and liberals alike critique communism because labour will cease and universal laziness will overtake us, this argument is the same argument the egoists and The Idler's Manifesto makes, but with more nuance and rhetorical ability. We do not make this argument lightly; nor is our purpose to restore liberalism and conservatism. Our purpose is to supersede communism. Secondly, we have found sufficient evidence that under communism, a form of wage-labour still exists, and hence, also a new form of capital. The only thing that has changed is the fixity of the wage, it is no longer a fixed number, but an unfixed number of needs for the individual; The relations of wage-labour, and capital exchange, between worker and society still exist.

Marx's only argument against universal laziness in communism is to compare the communist mode of production to the capitalist mode of production. They are not one and the same thing. His only argument is to claim that bourgeois society would have long ago vanished due to the sheer idleness of the bourgeoisie. The bourgeoisie can survive their own idleness and the idleness of the lumpen-proletariat because they have the state machinery to protect their interests. Through the grace of the state, they get certain political rights that give them the freedom to buy and exchange private property, these rights are protected and enforced by the state's machinery, the capitalist state is nothing but the henchman of capital, holding it up by, on the surface, a guise of manufactured consent, but, at its root, violence and authority. The bourgeoisie do not succumb to idleness because capitalism preys on, and capitalises on, the innate desire for Ownness, mutating it and conflating it with a never-ending desire for acclimation, which is then uses as a motivator to keep itself afloat; the unnecessary desire for acclimation is an inherent symptom of possession by the spectre of capitalism. Will communists succumb to universal laziness? Yes; because communist society has no state machinery to protect against the idler, and if it does build a state machinery anew, it is merely restoring socialism and destroying the statelessness of communism. The idlers do not succumb to their idleness because, so long as the serf-proletarian exists to create value for them; they will survive. The lumpen-proletariat of capitalism cannot increase their idleness; they seek to rejoin the working force because it is their only means of subsistence. The lumpen of future communist society can be sustained without joining the working force. Marx changes his allegiance from dialectics to tautology the moment he finds a dialectical process that challenges communism! The slogan of rebellion is no longer the socialist's cry "employment for all; not just the proletariat!" But has become the pauper's slogan of "Unemployment for all; not just the rich!"

For the communist, the disappearance of production, or productive labour itself; signifies the disappearance of all class culture; that culture which communists lament is but an outgrowth of the communist mode of production and public property; just as jurisprudence is but the will of the masses, which make up your class, and turn their interests into a law for all; a will whose essential character is determined by economic conditions of the existence of your class. The selfless misconception that induces the communists to transform dialectical materialism into metaphysical, eternal laws of nature and reason; the social forms springing from the communist mode of production and public property - historical relations that rise and vanish in the progress of production - this misconception you share with every ruling class that has preceded you. Once the communists have established communism, what need do they have for dialectical materialism to further transform society? They rid themselves of their ties to dialectical materialism, and like the bourgeoisie before them, turn back to metaphysics and eternal truths - the metaphysics of communist society as an eternal truth, static, experiencing no major changes. They rid themselves of dialectical and historical materialism as quickly as they picked it up. Their desire now is to preserve communist society; not destroy it - henceforth, the dialectic which was once a cornerstone of Marxist philosophy is immediately abandoned and is, in an attempt to preserve their society, replaced by metaphysics. Communism was described by Karl Marx in the following words:

'For as soon as the distribution of labour comes into being, each man has a particular, exclusive sphere of activity, which is forced upon him and from which he cannot escape. He is a hunter, a fisherman, a herdsman, or a critical critic, and must remain so if he does not want to lose his means of livelihood; while in communist society, where nobody has one exclusive sphere of activity but each can become accomplished in any branch he wishes, society regulates the general production and thus makes it possible for me to do one thing today and another tomorrow, to hunt in the morning, fish in the afternoon, rear cattle in the evening, criticise after dinner, just as I have a mind, without ever becoming hunter, fisherman, herdsman or critic'

Of course, our critics often use this quote to disprove the essence behind our manifesto as they ask us the sarcastic question, "how does this not fulfil the idler or the egoist? Is the egoist not already free in a communist society?" Not at all, because society regulates the general production, rather than I, it would be society that will tell me where my efforts are required and where they are not. If I own general production, it would be possible for me to do one thing today and another tomorrow without the interference of society This would fulfil me. Of course, Marx is under the assumption that communism is the last phase of history, where there are no longer any classes, and therefore, also no division of labour. But as we have shown; there are indeed new classes that struggle in communism, and with new classes also comes new divisions of labour between the mental and the physical.

In late-stage communism, there are two further stages of development for productive forces. The first stage is a semi-automated stage, and the second, the latest stage of communism, is a fully automated stage of the means of production. In the semi-automated stage, labour has not yet been replaced by automatons, and the labourers can engage in different spheres of activity; in the latest stage, automation has taken over all aspects of human labour, except for the maintenance of the means of production. Marx makes further incorrect statements about communism when he states:

'In a higher phase of communist society, after the enslaving subordination of the individual to the division of labour, and with it also the antithesis between mental and physical labour, has vanished, after labour has become not only a livelihood but life's prime want, after the productive forces have increased with the all-round development of the individual, and all the springs of co-operative wealth flow more abundantly--only then can the narrow horizon of bourgeois law be left behind in its entirety and society inscribe on its banners: From each according to his ability, to each according to his needs!'

This quotation might as well have been taken from *Der Einzige* itself, when Stirner said, 'Property, therefore, should not and cannot be abolished; it must rather be torn from ghostly hands and become my property; then the erroneous consciousness, that I cannot entitle myself to as much as I require, will vanish,' Stirner can be said to go further than Marx. In a higher phase of a pauper society, after the enslaving subordination of the individual to the division of labour - and with it also the antithesis between mental and physical labour has truly vanished - after labour has also, as a consequence, vanished, and property has become not only a livelihood: but life's prime want; after the productive forces have increased with the all-round development of the egoist, and all the springs of personal wealth flow more abundant – only then can the horizon of proletarian law be left behind, and the union of egoists be free to inscribe on its banner: 'From each according to his might; to each according to what he requires,' or as Max Alderbright, Head Propagandist of The EUI & South England Wing Founder, once put it, 'I am a man of my own means, and what I desire I will claim as my property. At the end of the world, when we all fall into our egoistic selves; He who wants, will have.'

In the quotation from *Critique of the Gotha Programme*, Marx would indeed be correct, if communism really meant the destruction of all classes and division of labour; but he would be incorrect if communism meant the rebirth of new classes and new divisions of labour. Communism has only temporarily done away with the enslavement of the division of labour, and the distinction between mental and physical labour. First and foremost, the idler does not idle away doing nothing for the rest of his days, he engages in unproductive forms of labour such as entertainment, being a flâneur, poet, artist, observer, philosopher, writer, photographer, musician, reader; he spends his days river-watching, star gazing and engaging in all such activities that are considered playful, enjoyable; have no productive value for society at large, but immense personal value for individual. The serf-proletariat engages in physical labour, the idler engages in mostly mental labour. Secondly in the latest stage of communism, the labourer is relegated to only one sole activity which communist society forces on the serf-proletarian in order to survive: the activity of supplying maintenance to the means of production. Physical labour has been divided into one sole monotonous activity, and therefore, the serf-proletarian starts to abhor physical labour as a most alienating experience and desires to become an idler, to seek a more fulfilling value from his labour which is found in mental labour. We must remember that the communist society of the future will inherit the means of production from our time - in our time, the means of production are already being automated; hence, future socialist states will adopt these means of production and keep them until communism.

The automated means of production require maintenance from the serf-proletariat, and in turn, the serf-proletarian requires that the means of production work properly so that it may supply him with food, furniture, resources, houses, and all the essential needs of life. Critics might argue that since the means of production are now efficiently controlled by automatons, the labourer will be free to do what he wants for the rest of the day. This is not the case, as the productive forces become so larger than life; that they also require a larger-than-life labouring force to maintain it. Marxism, therefore try as it may, is not a leisure theory but a labour theory. It is egoism that is the leisure theory that shall do away with the labour theory.

Marx and all the communists believe, like the utilitarians before them, that human needs can be measured quantitatively or mathematically; but desire and needs are immeasurable, that is to say limitless; no matter how large and fat the means of production are, they shall never satisfy the immeasurable needs of humanity. Henceforth the communist principle itself, 'to each according to our needs,' is a principle that destroys itself. Since my needs are limitless and immeasurable, I shall freely encroach on the needs of others and transform everything into my property. Thus, even the needs of others become my property - this characterises the idler's mode of existence in a communist society, as he survives through the transformation of other people's needs into his own. Once I have exhausted myself of desire for a while; I shall simply accommodate myself with myself, what Stirner called Self-enjoyment, until I feel hungry and desire the property of the rest of humanity once again. After this self-enjoyment stage, we start to inch closer and closer to the union of egoists' phase. The egoist, unlike the communist, does not attempt the folly of measuring himself for what he thinks he is owed or not owed. As

Stirner says, 'Man is the last evil spirit or spook, the most deceptive or most intimate, the craftiest liar with honest mien, the father of lies. The egoist, turning against the demands and concepts of the present, executes pitilessly the most measureless - desecration. Nothing is holy to him!' Therefore, the egoist also needs to execute pitilessly the most measureless desecration of the holy communist principle of measure, 'From each according to their abilities; to each according to their needs,' yet this measureless desecration commences from the inner contradiction within the communist principle that pits the measured against the measureless.

One might think that automation implies outright freedom from labour, but in actual fact, in order to maintain the billions of machines and automatons, the labourer is relegated to the activity of maintenance. The daily working hours will merely increase as automatons and machinery are increased in proportion. Society becomes a massive blob of grease, oil and machinery that needs constant maintenance. The division of labour therefore is the highest it has been in all of human history – workers being relegated merely to one sphere of activity. The only good news is, supposedly, communism is a stateless society. People can recognize the absurdity of labour, maintenance of the automaton machine and be transformed into idlers. The idlers are allowed free reign; there is no state machinery to stop them. They start to recognize, as Max Stirner said, that, 'they have run themselves tired, and are gradually noticing that "possession does not give happiness." Therefore, they are thinking of obtaining the necessary by an easier bargain, and spending on it only so much time and toil as its indispensableness exacts. Riches fall in price, and contented poverty, the care-free ragamuffin, becomes the seductive ideal.' What is Stirner talking about in this quote? He is talking about the idler who now seeks an easier bargain. Possession of property in communism does not please them; the mere possession of things wants to be replaced by owning things for yourself, rather than a simple use-value that is used by everyone. The communist workers only own the means of production so far, they find themselves in a collectivity of workers; he only possesses the means of production as an individual worker on the hour of work itself. He cannot uproot the machine from the factory and take it home with him, even in communism, this would be considered theft. Why theft? Because the means of production is owned by workers in the plural, not by individuals. Communism allows me to appropriate social products as my own, but not possess the means of production as my own as an individual, the best it can do is allow me to appropriate the means of production as a worker, and through that I, as an individual, become possessed by the masses.

The serf-proletarian sees no more worth in toiling long hours maintaining machines in communist society; he sees that society is already plentiful in abundant resources and that the means of production need little maintenance that they can provide his sustenance. The serf-proletarian ceases his labour; he extracts the wealth produced by the serf-proletarians and produces nothing in turn, thus transforming him into an idler. All this happens gradually, and the idler finds himself in an antagonistic relationship with the serf-proletarian.

The idler wants to become the sole master over the means of production as an Egoist Unique. He no longer longs for freedom from the labouring machines, but desires to own them for himself. Henceforth, the idler rises up in revolution, seizes the state machinery for himself as his own property towards the purposes of the abolition of labour rather than its glorification. Max Stirner took Descartes's notion of 'Cogito, ergo sum' - the famous phrase, 'I think, therefore I am' which he rejected on the grounds that the thinking-man was merely enhancing the dominion of thought upon the world. Stirner saw this phrase transformed by the communist proletarians when he remarks that 'Man is honoured only by human, self-conscious labour, only by the labour that has for its end no 'egoistic' purpose, but man, and is man's self-revelation; so that the saying should be 'laboro, ergo sum,' - 'I labour, therefore I am a man.' And now, with the complete abolition of labour and communist society, the egoist has mastered Ownness, so that the saying should be 'Meus sum ego, ergo sum Unicus,' - 'I am my own, therefore I am Unique;' or, 'I own, therefore I am Unique.' If I do not own, then I am owned; and if I am owned, I am but a fixed individual sacrificing myself at the altar of some spook; in other words, I do not recognize myself as Unique.

Abolition of Labour for Women! Women are the most natural idlers and have been for the major part of history, constantly shifting between working women and idlers. They understand better than men the notions of idleness. Modern women are becoming more and more aware that the so-called freedom to labour is merely the taking away of their freedom to be idle; in fact, one of my inspirations for The Idler's Manifesto has been my fiancé, who constantly drags herself from one coach to her bedroom, sleeping entire afternoons and idling her life away. What a truly admirable sight! That my beloved should be a better idler than I! No woman wants the drudgery of labour, they are the world's most natural idlers. This is our feminism. Labour under capitalism, due to the struggles of the working class, had already abolished labour for children, old people, the disabled, and for a time, even women; one could say more than half the population of the world was already idle. Capitalism, through its liberal feminism, sought to bring the female force back into the mechanism of labour and has altogether been a tragedy. After communism, in the Lumpen phase, women shall be our foremost and most dedicated idlers.

Friedrich Nietzsche, in his *Human, All Too Human*, remarked that the most remarkable and pardonable idler was indeed a woman. He defines her as 'The parasite - It denotes entire absence of a noble disposition when a person prefers to live in dependence at the expense of others, usually with a secret bitterness against them, in order only that he may not be obliged to work. Such a disposition is far more frequent in women than in men, also far more pardonable (for historical reasons).' The first division of labour was when a man needed a woman to aid him in his labour. It is only natural that a woman should be, therefore, the first to cease her labour altogether and lead that man towards the abolishment of labour.

Abolition [Aufhebung] of the masses! Even the most radical flare up at this proposal of the egoists. What you, as a communist, see clearly in the case of feudal property; what you admit in the case of bourgeois property, you are forbidden to admit in the case of your own communistic form of public property. It has always been the case that Marxists viewed sole individuals as insignificant throughout history; for them, history is driven by the masses, the masses become the new nuclear family, replacing the notion of bourgeois families. Among the stars that shine in the vastness of space, individual moments are insignificant; but also, the appearance of a single new star will change the map of all the heavenly bodies. Dear reader, are you a mere planet, or are you a new shining, unfixed star? On what foundation are the masses built? On communal capital, on public gain; not my personal gain as an egoist. In its completely developed form, these masses only exist among the communists. The masses will vanish alongside the vanishing of communal capital: the masses are distinct from society. Society has always existed in some shape or form, but the masses are mostly a phenomenon of modern industrial production. With capitalism, we see the rise of the masses as they are collected into the cities from the rural villages. In socialism and communism, the rise of the masses has reached its culmination. In egoism, it meets its doom. The masses did not always exist, and what did not always exist can perish by the same means it was brought about. The masses are a recent phenomenon which developed alongside capitalism as it constructed the industrial proletariat. The masses liberate themselves against capitalism in the socialist revolution. The masses are a necessary component for the construction of socialism and later communism, however, as time passes the inherent contradictions within communism would see the dissolvement of masses; the destruction of human labour through automation and the parasitic development of the idler classes slowly causes the destruction of the masses. The egoist mode of production which is introduced also helps in the destruction of the masses as an economic phenomenon. This makes it clear that the same economic phenomenon that brought about the existence of the modern masses as we know them will also bring about the destruction of the masses. The revolutionising of the means of production does not discriminate between outdated tools, outdated ideas, and the outdated industrial proletariat.

Long ago, religion was the opium of the people. Today, flavour of religion and opium has taken on the form of stale bread. The bourgeois idea of "people," or citizen, has always fallen out of favour and transformed into the proletarian idea of the "masses." Monotony is the spice of life for the lower classes; and what encapsulates the lower classes are the masses, and the industrial proletariat. The masses of critics unite their powers to vanquish the forces of egoism.

It is in fact quite an easy matter, as most of the time, we will not even have to raise a finger against them. The revolutionization of the means of production will destroy old tools, old conceptions, old labourers, old masters of history, the masses, monotony, and labour itself. Therefore, the masses can no longer remain the driving force of history since they have been vanquished from the annals of history; that responsibility now belongs to the ever-growing pauper class which, although numerous, is not part of the masses, but isolated into little pockets of society where they derive a miserable existence. Our understanding of the masses is not merely a population statistic, the word 'masses' refers to the economic phenomena that developed due to capitalism forcing the hand of agrarian workers to seek industrial labour in the greater industrial towns. Therefore, before the existence of capitalism, the masses as a phenomenon did not exist; nor did the industrial proletariat. The division of labour through automation cheapens labour. The task of the atomists has become to expand the returns to their own capital while reducing the cost of labour. The more labour value falls, the more people will be forced to sell themselves for cheaper labour and cheaper wages. The atomist can be a capitalist, he can be a socialist, and he can be a communist - if his goal is to expand abundance and social profit through automation, then he is an atomist. It is not only wages that will fall from grace, but also the value we put into our own families as a traditional unit, and as consequence also the masses themselves. What good will the mass line do you, o Maoist of the CCP, if there are no masses? That was a rhetorical question, you were not meant to answer that, foolish fellow. They might try to argue that the lumpenproletariat are now the heirs of the proletarian revolution as they now constitute the masses; however, the character of the lumpenproletariat is such that they are isolated from each other in life, and in labour, and therefore, can never constitute into a mass.

The further division of labour therefore will lead to a new consequence - mainly the division of the masses in the workplace and society at large. When labour is abolished; so are the masses in all aspects of life. The more labour is divided, the more the masses are isolated from each other which leads to aphasia, anxiety, speechlessness. People have lost the ability to organise union strikes because all they know in their life is isolation. After years of being stranded on an island, Robinson Crusoe could scarcely be recognized and found it difficult to communicate and reintegrate with his own people. So here we are now, the postmodern family, the dilemma of isolation, loss of communication, depression, fragmented families, fragmented labour, and fragmented masses. These postmodernists are so pessimistic that they no longer believe in the notion of struggle and revolution - they wallow within their shallow existence. Pessimism is one of those things I really hate, pessimism is brought about by itself, by pure inaction. The pessimist suffers from pessimism because he is a pessimist. If he were an optimist, there would be no pessimism, there would be an actual revolution.

The masses, as a thesis, are posited against the antithesis of the individual. The individual 'I' is annihilated alongside the masses forming in its place the union of egoists, which preserves elements from the masses and the 'I' within it. The union of egoists is a mass of people which belong to me as my property.

The union of egoists is a mass of people I can dispose of as I wish, since they are my property. The masses are scattered into egoist individuals who, every now and again, choose to associate with one another, but live a life mostly apart. 'We do not aspire to communal life but to a life apart.' The masses are no longer the agents of history, the individual is, of himself, all of history in his own development, going beyond what is Christian, humanist, and communist.

Since property and the means of production now belong to individual egoists, the means of production no longer force people to collect themselves in a cobble of masses in the great cities that capitalists and socialists create for the world of communism. When property becomes mine, the need for people to cobble up and unite together becomes less and less of a necessity. The Idler's State and its exploitation of surplus value leads to a surplus of idlers; the desocialization or individualisation of property given to each member of society continues to lead to a surplus of idlers and a decrease in serf-proletarians, henceforth, this dialectical change of quantity in the economic mode of communist production causes it to become transformed in quality as it changes into the egoist mode of production. With this transformation, the masses also gradually wither away as they are transformed into individuals. The masses have done their task, they lose their value as the masses and take comfort in themselves as The Unique. As Max Stirner remarks in *The Unique and Its Property*,

'Pauperism is the valuelessness of me, the phenomenon that I cannot realise value from myself. For this reason, state and pauperism are one and the same. The state does not let me come to my value, and continues in existence only through my valuelessness: it is forever intent on getting benefit from me, exploiting me, turning me to account, using me up, even if the use it gets from me consists only in mv supplying a prole (proletariat); it wants me to be 'it's creature.' Pauperism can be removed only when I as ego realise value from myself, when I give my own self value, and make my price myself. I must rise in revolt to rise in the world.'

Communism transforms me into a pauper. Communism is the valuelessness of me, the phenomenon that I cannot realise value from myself. For Stirner, enforced pauperism and the state are one and the same time, for him communism is yet another state that doesn't allow its serf-proletarians to come to their own value. Only when I as an egoist realise value from myself, when I give myself a self-value; only then will communism vanish; when my self-value as an egoist becomes contradictory to the pauperism of communist society. When the egoist gives himself his own self-value; he no longer requires the masses or other social classes to give him their value or a wage. No longer does he remain a pauper of the masses to preserve his existence; henceforth, the phenomenon of the masses is gradually abolished when the egoist comes into his own self-value. The masses are not eternal; history is not always made by the masses. As we can see clearly, the masses are a byproduct of their economic conditions and their mode of production. Change their mode of production, change their economic conditions, and the masses will cease to exist.

The Idler's Revolution is the most radical rupture with traditional communistic property relations. We therefore proclaim that the first step of the revolution by the idler class, is to raise their class from the level of the pauper to the position of the ruling class; to win the battle of dictatorships. The idlers will use their political supremacy to wrest communal capital away from serf-proletarian society. The idler's army will exploit and extract as much surplus value as it can, in fact, almost all the value produced by the serf-proletarians. The state of idlers is then responsible for enforcing that each serf-proletariat labours towards a particular purpose.

That purpose is namely one purpose: to use that extracted value first and foremost to scatter the means of production and dissocialize them. That extracted value at first becomes the state capital of the Idler's State. It is then used, as we have remarked, towards the purpose of scattering and dissocializing the means of production which, overtime, abolishes communal capital itself. Communal capital and communal labour annihilate themselves in a dialectic bringing about Ownness. In bourgeois society, capital was property of bourgeois idlers. In communism, communal capital is the public property of all. In egoism, capital is at an end because labour is at an end. All my efforts, all my individual labours (Which I own) go towards owning as much property through my might as much as possible. The labour that I own is not given up to a generality, society or the like; it is only something I enjoy and consume as my property. Every product I make, I regard as solely mine.

The dictatorship of the idlers is the antithetical opposite of the dictatorship of the proletariat. While that of the proletariat wanted to centralise the means of production in the hands of the state, the idler's dictatorship wants to decentralise the means of production, this basically means that each individual in society, every billionth member of society, takes his own means of production, his own little island or his own castle where he can rule as king; with all the amenities necessary to produce all manor of things, parcels of land, animals, and so forth. The idler's dictatorship is responsible for enforcing the serf-proletariat to develop automatons that are able to do most essential labour for them, until there comes such a time, when human labour is no longer a necessity as it has been replaced by automated labour. When this occurs, the idler's exploitation of the serf-proletarians' surplus value will become an absurdity. The serf-proletarian will say to himself, "Why do I continue to toil in the heat of the sun, when automatons have replaced human labour and when I can have a city for myself as an egoist master?" the serf-proletarian will cease his labour and henceforth, cease to exist as a social class. With the death of the serf-proletarian, the idler, who always relied upon the serf-proletarians' labour, also becomes extinct as a class, and alongside it, the state machinery and the dictatorship of the idlers also withers away. As Max Stirner said, in The Unique and Its Property:

'The labourers have the most enormous power in their hands, and, if they once became thoroughly conscious of it and used it, nothing would withstand them; they would only have to stop labour, regard the product of labour as theirs, and enjoy it. This is the sense of the labour disturbances which show themselves here and there. The state rests on the slavery of labour. If labour becomes free, the state is lost.'

According to Stirner in his book, the notion of freedom as opposed to Ownness means to get rid of. To get rid of the Tsar, the nobility, the monarch, the bourgeoisie, God, Church, State and so forth. In this context, Stirner also means that when we get rid of labour, hence, free from labour: it is then that the state is lost. The labourer must regard the product of his labour as his own product rather than the product of the bourgeoisie, or the product of a collective communist society. It is only when I regard the product as solely mine, that wage-labour and capital are totally made extinct. There are many egoists who fear that the state of the idlers will become authoritarian, in a sense of egoistically trying to preserve itself as a state. Perhaps it is true that a state, the epitome of an establishment of authority, will be authoritarian, yes; but due to the material conditions that bring this Idler's State into existence, and that dialectically steer the course it can take, the Idler's State cannot become authoritarian in the sense of oppressively ensuring its own longevity when it is a tool by which 'labour' is becoming free from enslavement. Labour becomes free when I, as an individual, can make it affordable for myself to labour with my own tools and for my own enjoyment - not for state, society, humanity and the like. At every moment in which, individual by individual, labour is becoming free from slavery - the state of the idler will wither away, it becomes lost. Meanwhile, the socialist dictatorship of the proletariat showed no signs of withering away, because the dictatorship of the proletariat rested on the slavery of labour, and as long as that existed, the state would not wither away. Even if eventually the dictatorship of the proletariat withers away as a result of freeing labour from the enslavement of the bourgeoisie; the state shall develop again based on the slavery of labour and the oppression from the proletariat upon the idler.

The Idler's Revolution is not carried out by a monolithic political party, but by a primitive union of egoists from the idler class. What is the difference therefore between the anarchist egoist and the authoritarian egoist? No difference at all! The only difference is that the anarchist does not believe he is being an authoritarian when in actual fact he is! This is the only difference. If anarchist egoists wanted to abolish the state machinery; they would still have to use their domination over the serf-proletariat in order to change the mode of production; in the end, they construct their own state of the idlers. Meanwhile, when the authoritarian egoist seizes the state machinery, he also uses the same type of domination over the labouring class.

The only form of property is my ability to own, and that includes things like my labour. The fact that I own my labour is clear because I can choose whether to utilise it or not. Marx is still haunted by the spooks of other forms of property such as private and public property; in reality, there is only one form of property. I own myself, and therefore, all things that come with myself, such as my labour and labour power. Marx argues that the proletariat have been made slaves of the bourgeoisie who have made themselves the owners of the material conditions of labour. Naturally for Marx, the solution is communism, whereby only labourers have made themselves the owners of the material conditions of labour. Such a communism liberates only the masses as owners of the material conditions of labour; I, as an egoist, become the slave of the masses, the true owners of these material conditions. The egoist, then, combats against communism. The egoist wishes to become the sole owner of the material conditions of labour; where he regards his product as his own property, rather than the property of a whole society. How is this accomplished? It is accomplished when the serf-proletariat ceases his labour and seizes the state that opposes him as his property in such a way that it no longer opposes him that I can regard freely my own product as my own property. The serf-proletariat therefore has to cease his own submissiveness in order to deal a blow to the communistic lordship of communist society.

Every state in existence is furnished by the means of production. When the means of production is given to the workers, we get communism: a stateless and classless society where the state machinery no longer owns the means of production as state and henceforth it withers away, it cannot furnish itself. As we have seen though, communism recreates class struggle anew. When then, the state machinery of the idlers has come into power, we must remember that the serf-proletariat at this point would have re-socialized or re-nationalized the industries. All the Idler's Union needs to do now is merely provide a means for the individuals comprising it to seize that means of production for themselves, one by one. When at last, everyone has taken his own means of production, the state can no longer survive, it has lost the thing which was furnishing its existence. Henceforth, rather than withering away, it will be egoing away. The state will dissolve into the ego and the union of egoists. The idler must transform his own valuelessness into something of worth, to impoverish the state itself so that it may wither away into egoism. The malnourishment of the state is the enrichment of me, the egoist, The Unique. The fall of the state invites me to my rise. As Max Stirner said in his famous quote:

'Therefore we two, the state and I, are enemies. I, the egoist, have not at heart the welfare of this 'human society.' I sacrifice nothing to it, I only utilise it; but to be able to utilise it completely I transform it rather into my property and my creature; that is, I annihilate it, and form in its place the Union of Egoists [Verein von Egoisten].'

I have always interpreted this quote by Stirner as him desiring to seize the state as his own property. How is Stirner supposed to utilise the state? Well first he has to own it as his property and creature, he must become a state owner. In order to become a state owner, he must first seize it through his might and force. What if individuals united together, seized the state, and decided to transform the mode of production into an egoistic mode of production? A state of idlers that uses the state machinery to ensure every single individual takes their own machinery to furnish themselves with their needs; with automation this is becoming more and more possible. Once the mode of production has been changed into an egoist economy, where every idler has been transformed into an egoist with his own property, machinery, means of production to furnish all his requirements, the state machinery that was previously transformed into our property and creature is annihilated, it is dissolved, there is no longer a need for it. It's replaced by a Union of Egoists. Not private property, not public property; but solely my personal property. Even David Leopold's Cambridge Edition of *The Ego and Its Own* states the following in its introduction:

'Stirner sees the state as a human product, albeit one that dominates its own creators. What generates and sustains the state, on his account, is the willingness of individuals to subordinate their own will to the 'will' of their own creation, expressed in law. Stirner's characterization of this relation between individual and state alludes, in its choice of vocabulary, to Hegel's dialectic of Herrschafi and Knechtschafi in the Phenomenology of Spirit: He who, to hold his own, must count on the absence of will in others is a thing made by these others, as the master is a thing made by the servant. If submissiveness ceased, it would be all over with lordship. (p. 175) But this promotion of Hegel's moment of 'recognition' in dominion into a complete account of the sources of state power results in what might be called an idealist sociology. The state exists only because of 'the disrespect that I have for myself' (p. 25 2), and 'with the vanishing of this undervaluation' the state itself will be 'extinguished' '

For Stirner, the state withering away is a material process, while for Hegel, it is an idealist sociology. Therefore, it is clear in this introduction to The Ego and Its Own that for Stirner, the state exists because I have a disrespect for myself, the state exists because I am a powerless pauper. Once I rise up in revolt, once I gain a newfound respect for myself as The Unique, as The Egoist, as the "Owner," rather than the pauper, then the state will no longer be respected; it will become a malnourished husk that disrespects itself.

Once this happens, under this undervaluation of the state, it will not simply vanish as the state, but be extinguished. In other words, the state will 'wither away' and dissolve into my egoism. Henceforth, far be it from Engels creating the idea that the state will wither away, it was Stirner who first made use of this term and the general idea that we must be egoists before we can be anarchists.

Before we can arrive at egoism, and the state can be dissolved, many measures must be taken in the Lumpen Phase by the Idler's Union: Let us give a summary of what procedures will be generally applicable:

1. Abolition of all public property and application of all property for individual purposes.
2. Abolition of the partitioning of society's wealth according to needs.
3. Partitioning only of the means of production themselves to furnish one's own needs.
4. Extraction of all surplus value as abundant resources for the state and its members; and the development of an idler's army to oversee that idler's interest are of the most prime importance.
5. Abolition of all rights; transformation into might.
6. Abolition of labour for all in a gradual manner
7. The development of automatons for each individual to take as his own property; extension of factories and instruments of production for each individual to own and run by himself with his automatons.
8. Equal opportunity of all to be idle and cease their labour.
9. Desocialization; individualisation of property and means of production.
10. Displacement, scattering, abolition of the masses.

11. Abolishment of any public or private education; the false
principle of education replaced with personal education
about oneself, self-learning. De-Spookification Camps for
the Spooks.
12. Gradual abolishment of communal capital and communal
wage-labour.
13. Development of the union of egoists; temporary unions to
replace the necessity of the Union of Idlers.

When, in the course of development, class distinctions have
disappeared, and all production has been concentrated in the
hands of individual egoists who choose then and again to
associate with other egoists, public power will vanish as a
political power, as an organised power of one class oppressing
another.

The idler, during its contest with the serf-proletarian, is
compelled, by force or circumstances, to organise itself as a class;
if, by means of a revolution, it makes itself the ruling class, and as
such sweeps away by force the old conditions of production, then
it will, along with these conditions, have swept away the
conditions for the existence of class antagonisms and of classes
generally; and will thereby have abolished its own supremacy as a
class. In place of the old communist society, with its classes and
antagonism, we have the union of the egoists, in which the
development of the Ownness of each is the condition for the
development of me as The Unique, since they also become my
property. They view me as their property and I view them as my
property. The proponents of egoism have hitherto interpreted The
Unique in various ways; the point however, is to change the point
into pointlessness and master Ownness. The Union of Egoists
fully comes into its own, leaving behind communist society.; each
single individual owning the means of production for his own
sustainment and luxury. In other words, without any stammering
or shyness, a Fully Automated Luxury Egoism. The ultimate goal,
henceforth, is the transformation of "the means of production"
into "the master of production" - the master of production will be
each and every individual as a master over his own means of

production; and no, this social reality does not equate to a petit-bourgeois's wet dream of having capitalist status and property. The master of production, the egoist, entitles himself to everything that is within his power to own which differs largely from being a petit bourgeoisie. The ultimate goal is autarky for each individual to be a master of himself, his own production and creativity. An aristocratic culture and life of self-sufficiency and self-reliance.

The last shades of spirit, religion, and humanism meet their end. The idlers and the serf-proletarian will meet their end. Dialectical materialism meets its end. The Revolution meets its end. Dialectical materialism is transformed into the creative nothing. Revolution is transformed into insurrection. From this nothingness, The Unique emerges.

As the great egoist Renzo Novatore in his book *Towards the Creative Nothing* remarked:

'Any society that you build will have its limits. And outside the limits of any society, unruly and heroic tramps will wander with their wild and virgin thought — those who cannot live without planning ever new and dreadful outbursts of rebellion! I shall be among them! And after me, as before me, there will be those saying to their fellows: "So turn to yourselves rather than to your gods and idols. Find what hides within you and bring it to the light; show yourselves!" Because every person who, searching his own inwardness, extracts what was mysteriously hidden therein is a shadow eclipsing any form of society which can exist under the sun! All societies tremble when the scornful aristocracy of tramps, inaccessible, unique ones, rulers over the ideal and conquerors of the nothing resolutely advances. So, come on, iconoclasts, forward! Already the foreboding sky grows dark and silent!'

The great successor of Egoism after Max Stirner, Renzo Novatore, continues to prove the claims of The Idler's Manifesto truthfully. The heroic tramps Novatore mentions are a vision of these future idlers who will cause the communist society to tremble at the aristocracy of the tramps. Why does Novatore call them Aristocrats? It is simply because the idler survives through the exploitation of the serf-proletarian in almost mediaeval fashion. The aristocratic tramp differs from the aristocrats of the Middle Ages since these tramps are owners of nothing, through which they create themselves. The darkness of Kali Yuga with a whip and sleigh rides on the maelstrom of the idlers, ushering in an eternal Mahapralaya, a great deluge and dissolution without end. Modernity is a wasteland. Novatore claims that anarchism is divided into 'two different philosophical concepts, the communistic and the individualistic, that divide it in the theoretical sphere' He claims that 'There are those (communists and individualists) who suffer - as Nietzsche would say - 'through an over-abundance of life, and those who suffer from the impoverishment of life.' However, Novatore, like Enzo Martucci and myself, recognize that these aspects are contradictions of each other. Communism, through its over-abundance of life, leads to the impoverishment of life because of the cheapening of everything including labour itself. Over-abundance cheapens everything; including itself, and thus, it runs that over-abundance is equivalent to impoverishment. The task of Novatore, and Martucci, and Hope is and was to overcome this division between anarchism and archism within the anarchist theoretical sphere. Novatore states that the only solution is a revolution. He claims that 'If a strong handful of rebels, higher people and heroes would be able to leap beyond the two currents of anarchism, suffering from vital over-abundance, to rally around the black flag of revolt, setting fire to the hearts of all the European nations, the old world would collapse' He furthermore claims in his essay, *The Anarchist Temperament in the Maelstrom of History*, that 'If this handful of daredevils will not leap out of the shadow to throw the black glove of defiance and revolt into the foul face of bourgeois society, the reptiles of political-hack demagoguery and all the speculating acrobats and hypocrites of human sorrow will remain the masters of the field, and over the tragic sun that seeks to enlighten the dark maelstrom of the sombre history that is passing, they will throw the obscene mask of white lead carried over the free horizon of human thought by that debauched clown named "Marx," and everything will end in a vile and grotesque comedy before which every anarchist should commit suicide out of dignity and shame.' Henceforth if Renzo Novatore were alive today, he would praise this manifesto as having 'overcome the two currents of egoist anarchism' which is archist and anarchist at the same time. At last, the final analysis has been accomplished. The tramps consolidate all their evil power in the underworld of amusements to assault the overworld of humanity. Away with this mad distemper of a lunacy they call humane love that strikes down both beggar and King! We have no further need for this Christened love! If, by rejecting my bequeathed rights and supporting my own might as an egoist, I shall contribute to save myself from the agonies of death attributed to some higher communist cause of freedom; or of some other revolutionary wisdom, equally fatal. If I can but be the instrument of preserving my own life and destroying everything that threatens my life. My own blessings and tears of transport, shall be sufficient consolation to me for the contempt of all mankind! But first we must acknowledge the age we live in: The Age of Man. We are living in the time of Man, where he alone reigns supreme. Man has become the new God after killing the old God of the heavens; this war against the heavens saw itself creating two kinds of men: the bourgeois man and the proletarian man. Eventually, the proletarian man, the creator of all values, came to be synonymous with Godliness, piety and the reformed Christian doctrine or Christianity without Christ. This was the communist ideal, the Marxist doctrine. Man, nowadays, is being transformed into his own opposite - the unman, the valueless pauper who creates nothing of worth.

The Age of Man is slowly coming to a close. As the curtains of this period in history close, the struggle between these two social classes reaches its peak, until one murders the other. As Nietzsche proclaimed long ago 'God is dead! God remains dead! And we have killed him!' Humanity has orchestrated this great murder and thought to itself 'Do we not ourselves have to become gods merely to appear worthy of it? There was never a greater deed -

and whoever is born after us will on account of this deed belong to a higher history than all history up to now!' But who is this man? Surely the most humane man is the proletariat, the creator of all things. But did we really kill God, asks Stirner? 'At the entrance of the modern time stands the 'God-man.' At its exit will only the God in the God-man evaporate? And can the God-man really die if only the God in him dies? They did not think of this question, and thought they were finished when in our days they brought to a victorious end the work of the Enlightenment, the vanquishing of God: they did not notice that man has killed God in order to become now - 'sole God on high.' The other world outside us is indeed brushed away, and the great undertaking of the men of the Enlightenment completed; but the other world in us has become a new heaven and calls us forth to renewed heaven-storming: God has had to give place, yet not to us, but to - man. How can you believe that the God-man is dead before the man in him, besides the God, is dead?' This is the question Stirner posits. While the fact that God is dead is a well-known fact, God cannot truly be dead, until man also is dead. The death of man shall be carried out by the unman, the inhuman being. The essence of which finds its climax in the struggle of inhuman paupers against the humane proletariat.   And now, if Man found enough courage to orchestrate the death of God, shall I not, as The Unique, and as the egoist, orchestrate the death of Man? Then I shall truly proclaim, 'Man is dead! Man remains dead! And I have killed him! There was never a greater deed - and whoever is born after me will, on account of this deed, belong to a higher history than all history up to now, their own history!' Do I not have to become God myself to appear worthy of this deed? So rises a new God - Me; or perhaps, "You," and a true God has no father. Harkening lightning cracks as it beckons for its Maker. The dispossessed recluse pariahs and outcasts await his commands. It beckons for him to lead a revolutionary army of flâneur vagabonds and hibernating hermits. An army of aristocratic Dionysian tramps, hedonistic harlot hoodlums, chandalas, criminals, convicts, coddiwomples, comprachicos, crooks, courtesans, cavalier servente, femme fatale, Mata Hari, exotic dancers, and vixen, fallen women or less savoury prostitutes. Junkie drunkards, gipsies, Romanian Ciocoii, Japanese hikikomori, forsaken Indo-Iranians, wandering Jews, nefarious barrel-scum prisoners, and inmate gangsters of ultra-violence. Thuggish warlords, thieves, tomb robbers, muggers, looters, beggars, burglars, bounty hunters, bums, highwaymen, hitmen, hucksters, poachers, peddlers, pickpockets and pirates. Vicissitudes, villains, voluptuaries knaves from supercratic satanic slums and sewers, rat-riddled with squatters, whoremasters, and godless, self-seeking tricksters. Debauchee lunatics of the greatest ghetto asylums in a state of eudaimonic Elysium. It beckons him to lead a motley crew of miscreant, motherless, Machiavellian, mass-murdering, marauding morticians and malevolent mafiosi; malicious, malignant, Mephistophelian mercenaries alongside a bedlam brigand berserker bandit band of noble barbarian war criminals and traitorous, back-stabbing, treacherous defectors of terrorism. The frenzied fringe-dwelling mavericks drifting in the dark of an eccentric night amongst the corpses of an oily, crow-infested graveyard where free thinking and phantasmic philosophy slips from the flimsy mind. They march forth to rid us of the red plague. The King of this Army of Whores accompanied by plague-ridden bubonic knights march in the darkest forests and swamps to pluck voluptuous virgins from the roots and rid the land of décadente communism. These idlers transform into the unique ones, rulers and conquerors of nothing. The Red Sun of the east grows dim, the clouds darken the skies. The age of heaven-storming is over; the age of mighty, reckless, shameless, conscienceless, proud – crime begins.

The sky is dark and silent!

3. EGOISM AND EGOIST LITERATURE

I. Reactionary Egoism

A. Feudal Egoism

Owing to their historical position, it became the vocation of aristocrats of France and England to be idle in their wealth. They are not egoists, but rather egotists, which means they are solely driven by idleness and selfish desire; but they are unconscious egoists nonetheless. The idler has many faces throughout history. The idler can be found in the ruling classes and also in the undesirable classes. Henceforth, the aristocrats, the nobility, and the bourgeoisie are all idlers, yet, in the same breath the majority of idlers per excellence is composed out of the ranks of the proletarians or labourers. feudalism had so many of these idlers, so many beggars and vagabonds, that monarchs executed them in the thousands. The feudal idlers of this time could be bought as tools by both the crown and the emerging bourgeoisie; hence, the idlers either became revolutionaries of the bourgeois kind or reactionaries protecting the crown. In this manner arose feudal egoism: half revolutionary; half reactionary. Being swindled by either the nobility or the emerging bourgeois class. Owing to their poverty, it doesn't take a genius to discover that the idlers of this time would have betrayed one class with another for a mere piece of bread. Yet, the idlers of feudalism are not as clear-cut as this.

Not all egoists and idlers could be easily pigeonholed either as revolutionaries or reactionaries. Some of them wanted to achieve a form of egoism. These fellows were mostly insurrectionists. One such group was the Brethren of the Free Spirit movement, which was a mystical and religious movement that emerged in Europe during the 13th and 14th centuries. The movement originated in the Low Countries (modern-day Netherlands, Belgium, and Luxembourg) and spread to other parts of Europe, including Germany and France.

The movement emphasised the immanence of God, believing that God resided within every individual, and that the distinction between the divine and human was illusory. In one way, this is an anticipation of Ludwig Feuerbach's *Essence of Christianity*. They promoted the idea of "libertinage" or spiritual liberty, which meant living in complete freedom from societal norms and moral constraints. This, in turn, could be seen as an anticipation of Max Stirner's Ownness, to master oneself in a manner in which one can no longer be controlled via societal norms and moral constraints. The Brethren of the Free Spirit was considered heretical by the catholic church at the time and many were persecuted by the ruling class until they vanished in the 15th century. They practised communal living and, like wandering vagabonds, moved from one location to another. They were characterised by four essential beliefs: namely, Antinomianism, the pure rejection of traditional morality imposed by society or the church, and furthermore, their belief that if one achieved spiritual perfection, they would no longer be bound by Mosaic law, and henceforth, free from any sin. This meant that they could practise sexual liberation, indulging in hedonistic activities while still believing themselves to be free from sin. Their spiritual libertinage included complete freedom from societal laws and the practice of sexual freedom, as well as other forms of freedom. They rejected church authority as an institution and instead practised prayer, meditation, and asceticism in pursuit of Mystical Ecstasy. This association of bohemian vagabondish Christians could be considered the first proto union of egoists. Another sort of association at his time was the Beguines and Beghards which emerged way back in the 12th century. The Beguine movement generally experienced a longer duration compared to the Beghards. Beguine communities continued to exist in parts of Europe well into the 16th and 17th centuries. In some regions, such as the Low Countries, (modern-day Belgium, Netherlands, and Luxembourg), beguinages persisted until the 19th century. How come the idlers had associations before the earliest proletariat had their own associations such as the True Levellers or the Diggers movement? This is because the idler has always existed, in some shape or form, in every era of history, and each era of history has a union of idlers with different conditions. A later association of vagabonds would be the organisation of beggars that was established in Vilnius, Lithuania in 1636, and operated there until 1784. This organisation was like a guild for beggars, henceforth this organisation would fall under the category of feudal practising egoists.

The Beguines and Beghards were not allowed to marry once they found themselves in this association, they lived a life of devotion, outside the sphere of labour, living through prayer and begging alone. Another rule of their association was that they were free to leave the association as soon as it no longer suited their personal interest, in similar ways, this is also a proto union of egoists with vagabonds in its midst. It allowed its members the freedom to join and leave the union at any point in time. However, as an association they were predominantly very Christian, still haunted by the spook of sin. The Beguines and Beghards were not advocates of antinomianism like the Brethren of the Free Spirit which saw its ultimate decline in the 15th century. The Brethren of the Spirit was more like an actual union of egoists because it was no longer haunted by the spooks of morality, sin, ethics. They appropriated everything they saw fit for consumption and personal ownership through force and might.

Although they vanished in the 15th century, another form of association of idle egoists would later form again under a different name during the 17th century that was almost an exact copy of the Brethren of the Free spirit. History repeats itself yet again under different conditions. The idlers associate again in a union, this time, with less mystical freedom on the forefront of their agenda and instead a focus on a revolt against feudal society. The Brethren of the Free Spirit were mainly concerned with mysticism; while the Ranters during the English Civil War and the Interregnum (1642-1660) were more concerned with political dissent and radicalism. The Ranters held the same beliefs as the Free Brethren. It is a case of the negation of the negation, the return to origins under different conditions. The Ranters, with their Antinomianism believed that God was immanent inside each member of society and therefore rejected the notions of sin and salvation, believed that all actions were permissible so long as they were divinely inspired. Even normally considered sinful acts such as hedonistic sexuality, theft, murder, and so forth. They rejected the notion of an afterlife after death and believed in the divinity of the moment. In this manner, they could be called yet again to the podium anticipating Max Stirner. Unfortunately, the manner in which they come to the conclusion that they are egoists is not through the negation of idealism or materialism but through God. In this manner, feudal egoism is a union of idlers in a mixture and motley crew of Feuerbachian, Stirnerian, and Christian Egoism. It is what Max Stirner described in The Unique and its Property, as the involuntary, or, unconscious egoist.

The Brethren of the Free Spirit and the Rafters are therefore these involuntary egoists who always combat their inner egoism and abases himself to cease being an egoist, but by looking about in heaven or earth to serve higher beings for his own sake, he exalts himself yet again as an egoist. This early union of idlers and egoists did everything a vagabondish egoist would do but only in the name of higher things than themselves, God or Spirit. Their acts of egoism were merely actions of divine inspiration. I stole food like a vagabond because of inspiration of God, I engaged in acts of incest with my half-sister because of divine inspiration. They affirm their egoism through the divine and hence the divine gains a primary importance over their ego. Voluntary egoists negate the divine in order to affirm their egoism. They managed to somehow, transform God into an altogether immanent entity, in a manner that they reduced the distance between themselves and God; in such a manner that the divine was not altogether different from themselves. Yet, when these fellows found themselves face to face with the world, they had to shed their idealism in exchange for materialism. Their idealism was incompatible and in contradiction with the evolution of the world.

This is what we may call clerical egoism which was predominant in the feudal era. In the same manner, feudal socialism was plagued by a tinge of Christian socialism. The Brethren of the Free Spirit, The Rafters, The Beguines and Beghards, are all forms of concealed egoism. As Max Stirner says in *The Unique and Its Property*:

'Even religion, therefore, is founded on our egoism and - exploits it; calculated for our desires, it stifles many others for the sake of one. This then gives the phenomenon of cheated egoism, where I satisfy, not myself, but one of my desires, such as the impulse toward blessedness. Religion promises me the - 'supreme good'; to gain this I no longer regard any other of my desires, and do not slake them. - All your doings are unconfessed, secret, covert, and concealed egoism. But because they are egoism that you are unwilling to confess to yourselves, that you keep secret from yourselves, hence not manifest and public egoism, consequently unconscious egoism, therefore they are not egoism, but thraldom, service, self-renunciation; you are egoists, and you are not, since you renounce egoism.'

Religion for Max Stirner is not merely the religion of Gods but also of humanism, politics, it is anything that I as an individual must swear fealty towards. Henceforth, even liberalism and communism are a form of religion, the humane religion. Religion for Stirner is therefore like the bourgeoisie of our egoism, it extracts the surplus value of our egoism. Even in communist society, for the egoist, this society is like the bourgeoisie who extracts the surplus value of our egoism and henceforth builds itself out of our egoism. In the same manner, the bourgeoisie build their wealth upon the extraction of surplus value from the fruits of labour generated by the proletariat. It is likewise that communist society is built out of our egoism which is exploited by it, taken away from us. The communists are egoists, yet they are not at the same time, since they renounce their egoism. This is the ultimate critique against those who call themselves egoist-communists, who attempt to somehow reconcile egoism with communism. These include for instance, the Situationists in their book, *Right to be Greedy*, Emma Goldman who synthesised Stirner with Kropotkin, Friedrich Engels, who was awestruck and already adapting his theories of communist to egoism shortly after finishing Stirner's book before being scolded by Marx and abandoning the ideas; and even Friedrich Engels himself who somehow found a way to reconcile his egoism with communism.

How does it stand with the communist masses, whose cause are we to make our own? Is its cause that of another and do the communist masses serve a higher cause? No, Communism sees only itself, the masses will promote the interests of the masses only, the mass itself is its cause. That it may develop, it causes nations and individuals to wear themselves out in its service, and, when they have accomplished what communism needs, it throws them on the dung-heap of history in gratitude. Is not the communist and the masses' cause - a purely egoistic cause? But of course, if I state this, then such a thing as Engels's Egoist Communism would be possible? Not if I follow what Max Stirner says next: that the egoist will learn from these great egoistic institutions that serve their own cause, such as mankind, communism, or God. Stirner specifically states 'I for my part take a lesson from them, and propose, instead of further unselfishly serving those great egoists, rather to be the egoist myself'

This sort of egoist communism is not at all compatible with Max Stirner's egoism. In communistic egoism, only the impulse towards labour is satisfied, only the communistic tendencies of your 'egoist communism' are being acknowledged. The "egoist" who calls themselves an egoist-communist, or any other suffix of egoism, is actually belittling their uniqueness by adding that suffix; the egoist is free to make out of himself anything he wishes in any moment without restriction, adding a suffix is only limiting. It is a cheated egoism, I self-renunciate myself to communist society and allow communist society, to have a monopoly upon all my reserves of egoism, lets me only be egoist so far as I am a loyal labourer of communism. It is not so different from capitalism, where the proletariat is forced to sell his labour and give up his surplus value to generate profit for the bourgeoisie: in communism, yet again, I am forced to sell my labour and give up my surplus value to generate profit for the rest of communist society.

Already Engels speaks of egoism as a virtue! It is horrendous! He transforms my cause as an egoist into the cause of collectivity. Engels therefore is not an egoist but a cheated egoist. He is an egoist and at the same time he is not. This is the major criticism egoists have against communist egoists and those fellows from *The Right to be Greedy* who quite simply repeat the same thing Friedrich Engels claimed but at much more length. This is nothing short of a new humanist religion. We are therefore in agreement with Lawrence S. Stepelevich, the Scholar of the Young Hegelians who states:

"Among others who shared the "new discovery" of Man would have been Karl Marx. At the time that time that the Ego appeared was considered a devoted follower of Feuerbach, and had even set about writing a work based upon Feuerbach's Philosophy of the Future. It is not insignificant that Bruno Bauer, the "Messiah of Atheism" was Marx's friend and teacher during Marx's brief student days in Berlin. They had not only planned a Journal of Atheism, but both had studied the Book of Isaiah. This Old Testament work is a gathering of oracles, prophecies, and reports with one common theme: the coming of a Messiah to save the oppressed. It is not unimaginable that Marx, who had descended from a long line of Rabbis, might well have considered himself the new Messiah, one bent upon the salvation of the poor downtrodden Proletariat and leading them into a heavenly, if earthly, "Classless Society." The idea that Marxism was in essence a religion was first presented by Stirner, and it later developed into an accepted view. On this, at a later time, Bertrand Russell found himself in agreement with Stirner when it came to taking communism as a theological doctrine:

The Jewish pattern of history, past and future, is such as to make a powerful appeal to the oppressed and unfortunate at all times. St. Augustine adapted this pattern to Christianity, Marx to Socialism. To understand Marx psychologically, one should use the following dictionary: Yahweh = Dialectical Materialism; The Messiah = Marx; The Elect = The Proletariat; The Church = The Communist Party; The Second Coming = The Revolution; Hell = Punishment of the Capitalists; The Millennium = The Communist Commonwealth?"

Religion, especially the Abrahamic religions, are based upon the eternal war against good and evil. This goes even beyond Judaism with Zoroastrianism. The dualism between good and evil is introduced with the Prophet Zarathushtra and these forces engage in an eternal war against each other. When one reads those scriptures, one notes how awfully similar they are to the communist manifesto, with an "eternal enemy in the bourgeoisie" after all, for any religion to spread, it needs a devil, or the evil one. Are the paupers therefore also a religion? After all, do we not also have an enemy in the proletariat? The answer, in a simple manner, is no, that we are on the verge of exorcising religion once and for all; the goal is to overcome religion and these dualities. The paupers will exist whether the egoists want them to or not. Each and every pauper can escape his own pauperism through struggle and become an egoist. The egoists on the other hand who are in the growing minority have already escaped this struggle, have beaten religion already and therefore have gone beyond good and evil, have gone beyond proletarianism and pauperism. Are we therefore following the same Jewish pattern of History? Are we using the following dictionary: Dialectical Materialism = Creative Nothing; The Messiah = Max Stirner; The Elect = The Paupers; The Church = The Idler's Union; The Second Coming = The Insurrection; Hell = Punishment of the Proletarians; The Millennium = The Union of Egoists? The answer to this question is that we are not following this same pattern - but rather we are doing a countermovement to this pattern. There is no Messiah, each and every single one of us is his own saviour; and since there is no Messiah, there is therefore no elected people or chosen people. Since there are no elected people, there is no church, and since there is no church, no one can lead the second coming. And without a second coming to seek out justice, there can be no Hell.

And if there is no Hell, there can be no heaven and therefore no Millennium.

Each and every unique person will have to seek his own salvation or damnation or settle for none of these things. The egoism of Stirner can therefore never be a religion in itself; although the paupers who slowly transform themselves into egoists can have religious elements out of which they are struggling to break free.

If there ever was a countermovement against the Prophet Zarathustra who the age of the later Abrahamic religions, it would be none other than Friedrich Nietzsche. Zarathustra introduced good and evil; Nietzsche went beyond them. If there ever was a countermovement against Christ, it would be none other than Max Stirner. While Christ came to complete the law; Stirner came to abolish it. Across history there were others who sought to abolish the law and the notions of good and evil, such as the Brethren of the Free and the Ranters.

The Brethren of the Free and the Ranters, although very radical in their approach, still ultimately resort to self-renunciation; but for them this renunciation was also a self-affirmation of their egoism. The Brethren and the Ranters are closer to actual egoism than any other religious denomination or political belief. They are more egoist than the communists in this regard because through the divine, they reached an egoism unprecedented by any other movement. The Brethren in particular do not renounce God or negate him like Stirner, but rather they bring God down their own level, to the point where they no longer believe in sin and that they have already been saved. The fact that they believe this means that they now renounce the need for self-renunciation to God himself; they do not need to follow the law of God or God's morality, they consider themselves already saved people by God. Henceforth, because they no longer required salvation from sin; they are free to do whatever they want, everything is permissible. They act like egoists; they are egoists and they do not renounce themselves like other Christian denominations or the humane religious sphere. Their only flaw is that they are idealists and that they believed that the spirit moved through them; acted through them in an almost Hegelian fashion. Henceforth, they give credit of their egoism yet again to spirit rather than their own potential as unique ones.

Nothing is easier than to give Christian asceticism an egoist tinge. Christian egoism is but the holy water of the catholic laymen that transforms him into a protestant or a puritan. There have been many so-called egoists who found similarities between the mysticism of the feudal ages and the egoism of Max Stirner. While it is true, that there are many similarities between Taoism, Advaita Vedanta (Non-Dualism) of Adi Shankara, the early ancient egoistic branch of Yangism from the philosophy of Yang Zhu, Master Zhuangzi's book, Zhuangzi or Lao Tzu's *Tao Te Ching* and other forms of mysticism - the mystics are to be considered as amongst the first of vagabonds who delve into the philosophy of egoism, yet remain idealists rather than materialists, remain metaphysicians rather than dialecticians, and therefore, unscientific. Such egoist feudal mystics have reached a level of a conscious egoism which remains an involuntary egoism. There remains a large gap between the involuntary egoism of the mystics, and the voluntary egoism of The Unique. That being said, alongside the heroics of Renzo Novatore, there are also the heroic acts of the involuntary egoist Marguerite Porete, a mystic in the beguine movement of the 13th century who was burnt at the stake for her mystical writings such as The Mirror of Simple Souls. Marguerite Porete saw everything in the world as God, and the individual will have to be given up for God's will, which was the will of herself and of all things. However, in so doing, she hath become God, and since she was God, she was as unique as God - as egoistic as God, and no quality could describe her since she had become God who had no more need of law or morality; free from the shackles of sin. Her union is not a union of egoists amongst egoists, but rather, a union with herself as an egoist and God as an egoist. Yet, it remains an involuntary conscious egoism, still holding fast to God - while claiming that God and I are one and the same essence; Porete still gives up her individual will to God's will.

The mistake is two-fold. The argument that my essence and that of God are the same, and the argument that my will and God's will are one and the same. Porete's mystical egoism differs from modern egoism by these facts. A modern egoist would argue that I am like God, in that no word can fully describe or extinguish me, but my essence and that of God is different, and our wills are also different. There are many parallels with Marguerite Porete and Dora Marsden in her later egoist writings. As opposed to the Mystics, there are also the hedonistic materialistic egoists who, although are materialists, are crude materialists still bound by metaphysics. For instance, the Epicureans or the Hindu Charvaka philosophy, these adhere to the pleasure principle; their egoism remains an involuntary egoism and when it is a voluntary egoism, it is an unconscious egoism - adhering to pleasure for the sake of pleasure, rather than for the sake of oneself, one which still believed in a morality, and the highest human good. What these ancient egoist philosophies prove is that egoism as a philosophy has seen a lot of developments in history until there came such a time when it regards itself no longer as a philosophy but precisely the thing which abolishes philosophy.

The most despicable act an egoist can take is self-sacrifice for a cause one considers higher than one's own. Stirner concludes, that all the higher causes, be it God, religion, truth, morality, the cause of fatherland, mankind, humanism, virtues, liberty, equality, fraternity, the communist cause and the like, are quite selfish indeed that they must demand my self-sacrifice for their own "sake." I shall follow their example and be as selfish as these higher ideals are, so that these causes find their death in me, rather than I find my death in them. These ideals should thereby sacrifice themselves for my sake, rather than the other way round. How do we bring about this reality of sacrificing these so-called higher ideals for my sake on my own altar? Through nothing more than the tempestuous revolution of the vagabonds of the great IDEA as Novatore had revealed years ago.

The head of this school is the French mutualist anarchist Pierre-Joseph Proudhon, who Max Stirner critiqued with a passion in the follow extract from *The Unique and Its Property:*

'Property as the civic liberals understand it deserves the attacks of the communists and Proudhon: it is untenable, because the civic proprietor is in truth nothing but a propertyless man, one who is everywhere shut out. Instead of owning the world, as he might, he does not own even the paltry point on which he turns around. Proudhon wants not the proprietaire but the possesseur or usufruitier.' What does that mean? He wants no one to own the land; but the benefit of it - even though one was allowed only the hundredth part of this benefit, this fruit - is at any rate - one's property, which he can dispose of at will. He who has only the benefit of a field is assuredly not the proprietor of it; still less he who, as Proudhon would have it, must give up so much of this benefit as is not required for his wants; but he is the proprietor of the share that is left him. Proudhon, therefore, denies only such and such property, not property itself. If we want no longer to leave the land to the landed proprietors, but to appropriate it for ourselves, we unite ourselves to this end, form a union, a societe, that makes itself proprietor; if we have good luck in this, then those persons cease to be landed proprietors. And, as from the land, so we can drive them out of many another property yet, in order to make it our property, the property of the - conquerors. The conquerors form a society which one may imagine so great that it by degrees embraces all humanity; but so-called humanity too is as such only a thought (spook); the individuals are its reality. And these individuals as a collective mass will treat land and earth not less arbitrarily than an isolated individual or so-called proprietaire.'

Proudhon wanted to elevate the proletariat to the level of the bourgeoisie, but in doing so, he merely wished for a bourgeoisie without the proletariat. Perhaps, due to the Automative

Revolution, we might see his vision come true, but not at all in the manner by which was intended by him. In the future communist society, the petit-bourgeois serfs will no doubt be Proudhonists reawakened from the dirt. The communists in the eyes of Stirner are not so different than Proudhon in stating the following:

'On the contrary, what man can obtain belongs to him: the world belongs to me. Do you say anything else by your opposite proposition? 'The world belongs to all?' All are I and again I, etc. But you make out of the 'all' a spook, and make it sacred, so that then the 'all' become the individual's fearful master. Then the ghost of 'right' places itself on their side. Proudhon, like the communists, fights against egoism. Therefore, they are continuations and consistent carryings-out of the Christian principle, the principle of love, of sacrifice for something general, something alien. They complete in property, only what has long been extant as a matter of fact - namely, the propertylessness of the individual.'

We are therefore forced to admit that every reactionary form of egoism is essentially a social egoism by which the individual becomes fettered by the fearful master of society, the consistent carrying-out of the Christian principle of love and self-sacrifice. We are therefore forced to admit also that The Idler's Manifesto represents a certain danger when we ask ourselves, what of the idlers and the Idler's Revolution? Is the cause of the Idler's Revolution also a spook, carrying out the Christian principle of love and self-sacrifice? We must, without any reservation, say that indeed: the idler's Revolution and the cause of the idler is not my cause as an egoist; it is the cause of social idlers. It is henceforth also a spook. However, unlike the cause of liberals or communists, the cause of the idler is always in the process of transforming itself into my cause as an egoist. The idlers have always been a class that has obtained whatever the world has thrown at it. Each and every idler sees the world as something that belongs to him. Henceforth, although the idler is a spook, he is the closest to being an egoist. The world must first be covered in the rags of the ragamuffin before it can be transformed into the unique one. The idlers experience inner contradiction within themselves; on one hand they serve the cause of the idlers, and on the other hand, they are transforming into egoists, serving only themselves. The idler of communism is an interesting phenomenon, becoming an egoist for a spur of a moment, then reverting back into his old lumpen self. The idler has to overcome his rags and his ragamuffin state as a pauper of communist society and emerge from this struggle an egoist. The socialism of the USSR did not defeat all the elements of the old society, the idlers, in the same manner, cannot defeat all the elements of their old selves immediately in their revolution against communism. Once they do however, they can call themselves egoists who serve only their cause and not the cause of the idlers. The idlers develop throughout history, at one point they are Christian, at another point they are vagabonds, petit-bourgeoisie, and Proudhonist, at another point they may even associate themselves with communism, but they remain idlers, not egoists.

C. German, or 'True,' Egoism

This refers to the egoist literature that originated in the early 20th century under the pressure of the workers and in power, and that was the expression of the struggle against this power; introduced into France for the first time during the events of the Paris Commune, and later on introduced into Germany at a time when the proletarian in that country had just begun its contest with bourgeois absolutism during the Spartacist uprising. German would-be egoists eagerly seized on this literature, not forgetting that when these writings immigrated from France into Germany, French social conditions had not immigrated along with them. The conclusion was a synthesis of political anarchism and egoism, for instance, the Scottish-German John Henry Mackay who, although did an excellent job as a biographer of Max Stirner, always thought that egoism and anarchism were synonymous. Another development of True German Egoism developed later under Adolf Brand, but fell to Masculinist tendencies. However, ever since Mackay's biography and his assertion that egoism is a form of anarchism, the idea stuck, later egoists adopted this idea, even Renzo Novatore. With time, Novatore gave new definitions to his anarchism which escaped those of Bakunin and Kropotkin, transforming Novatore into one of the first leading scientific egoists. Renzo's anarchism is not the same as the anarchism of Mackay and the True German Egoists. Novatore's anarchism is both Archist and Anarchist at the same time. It is not only Ernst Jünger, Dora Marsden, Sidney Parker that refer to themselves as Archist Egoists, but also the Italian egoist and great friend of Renzo Novatore, Enzo Martucci who wrote an essay called In Defence of Stirner where he quite clearly states that egoism is neither anarchist not archist, but both. Martucci says, 'However, the question between anarchists and archists has been badly stated from the beginning. In fact, we are not concerned with whether anarchy or archy can cement the best social relations, or bring about the most complete understanding and harmony between individuals. We try, instead, to discover which is the most useful for the realisation and expression of the individual—who is the only existing reality. Is it anarchy, which offer me a free and perilous life, in which I might fall from one moment to another, but which allows me to affirm myself at least once? Is it archy, which guarantees me a controlled life in which I am confined and protected, but in which I can never live as I feel and will? Which is preferable—intensity or duration? Michelstaedter has said that preoccupation with tomorrow limits living. I am for today.' In other words, not only does Martucci acknowledge the divide between anarchists and archists, but now he seeks to unite them in one as inseparable. For Martucci, being an archist egoist or an anarchist egoist depends solely on what I want today. Today I may want the intensity of anarchism, tomorrow I may want the duration of the Idler's Revolution, the Idler's State, the archism of the egoist and so forth. I am not preoccupied with tomorrow, even in the duration of the state. Today I take actions, I can only presuppose about the future but cannot predict it or worry myself over it. Martucci continues his quote by his criticism of John Henry Mackay, who believed only in anarchism rather than archism, that they were two different separable isolated things rather than a united thing through the unity of opposites. Enzo

Martucci critiqued them as 'The sheep, even if they call themselves anarchists, long for tomorrow. And they die waiting for the sun of the future to rise. To the anti-Stirnerism of the bourgeoisie, the Marxists and the libertarian socialist (Bakuninists, Kropotkinists, Malatestaians) must be contrasted the pseudo—Stirnerism of John Henry Mackay and E. Armand. Pseudo-Stirnerism gives us a sweetened Stirner who tends towards the same end as the libertarian socialists — that is social harmony. But they do not think it can be achieved, as do the latter, by means of Bakunin's impulse to unity or Kropotkin's mutual aid, but rather through individual egoism. In order not to be attacked by others and have my life and freedom threatened, [respect the life and freedom of others. it is not from love of my neighbours that I do not look for well-being in their suffering, but from personal interest.' Henceforth, although John Henry Mackay may have been an excellent historical biographer of Max Stirner, he used his power as a historical biographer of Stirner in order to subvert Stirner's message into a sort of 'Pseudo-Stirnerism' where by which, the egoism of Stirner could be pigeon-holed within the anarchist tradition of socialism alone. They give us a sweet Stirner, not the hard brutal cold Stirner. It is exactly the same thing the modern Egoist-Communists try to accomplish today. The situationist fellows behind Right to be Greedy and Jacob Blumenfeld, all give us the sweet egoist Stirner in which a communist society is very possible. This trend of obscuring what Max Stirner was talking about started first with Mackay, continued with Benjamin Tucker, and later on continued with the situationists and the modern egoist-communists. The modern egoists of today have been influenced by these Pseudo-Stirnerians, so that every egoist today have either forgotten about the egoist archists of the past, or are taught to scorn them. Enzo Martucci himself noticed that this was already happening in his own time, and agrees as much when he says, 'Certain authors confuse individualism with utilitarianism, Stirner with Bentham, the personal pleasure of the unique one with that of the majority or even of all. And they write works like Mackay's *The Anarchists and Armand's L'initiation individualiste anarchiste* which certainly do not contribute to the understanding of real Stirnerian thinking.' - The same could be said about the situationists' *The Right to be Greedy* and Jacob Blumenfeld's *All Things are Nothing to Me*. In other words, Martucci, being a very well-read fellow and clearly familiar with the works of Engels and Marx, specifically *The German Ideology*, knew that Stirner was often confused with Bentham. One of the first mistakes that Engels makes is in one of his letters to Marx, Stirner's unique self-enjoyment is confused with the enjoyment of the majority, that is why a trend such as egoist communism was able to construct itself.

The egoist Sidney Parker, in his essay *Archists, Anarchists and Egoists*, quotes John Henry Mackay and Max Stirner to highlight their essential differences, to highlight the fact that Mackay was an anarchist and Stirner a living synthesis of the two: Mackay says "I am an anarchist! Wherefore I will not rule and also ruled I will not be." While Max Stirner, the opposite, when he says, "What I get by force I get by force, and what I do not get by force I have no right to." Martucci and Parker use the unity of opposites, whereby I am both anarchist and archist, and they claim, rightfully so, that this is Stirner's position.

This individualist anarchism and archism of Renzo Novatore, Enzo Martucci, and even the heroic 19-year-old egoist Italian poet Bruno Filippi, spread like wildfire and egoists started calling themselves anarchists. Nowadays, every egoist is some form of anarchist and they call this the only 'True Egoism' - any other form of egoism that is slightly authoritarian in nature for them is unacceptable. Some of these True egoists reject Stirner's notion of class struggle between the ragamuffin labourer and the leisure-enjoying idler, they reject Stirner's dialectical egoism, they reject Stirner's domination in favour of equality among men, and finally, they reject any revolution in favour of insurrection, but when the time comes for them to show us what they are capable off; they fall back into words and no action takes place because they are spineless cowards. It's true that Stirner says we must not set any glittering hopes for institutions, and that the revolution sets for new arrangements; The Idler's Revolution is a set of new arrangements, but will later allow the opportunity for each egoist to arrange himself as he sees fit. Furthermore, Stirner advocated insurrection only after he had finished his dialectical analysis of the class struggle between the idler and the labourer; in other words, the revolution will be waged by idlers, not fully fledged egoists, they will engage in a revolution that will give the arrangements necessary for one to transform himself into an insurrectionist. It is once this stage is achieved, that the insurrectionary egoist can flourish in his best environment.

The only thing these 'True Egoists' own is their mouths, and, in proclaiming that they are unique, they are merely comforting themselves with this fact while being owned by a myriad of spooks that restrict the full potential of their Ownness. What use is my uniqueness if I am a spineless wretch? What use is the fact of my uniqueness, if it's pale, weak, and cowardly? They disregard any violent actions against the state because it's in their selfish interest not to get into trouble with the authorities - while in fact they are recognizing them as authorities over themselves in saying such things. Such a passive egoism serves merely the interests of the bourgeoisie, the petit-bourgeois class, and even the proletariat class. It is unfortunate, but the True Egoists are adorned with the robe of speculative cobwebs, embroidered with the flowers of rhetoric, steeped in the dew of sickly sentiment about one's own uniqueness. These 'True Egoists' lastly disregard's Stirner's idea that one should transform the incorporeal spook into one's own corporeality. They also misunderstand Stirner's theory of spooks and think spooks are mere illusions of spirit. Stirner knew that a spook has a two-layer reality, the spiritual, or metaphorical reality, and the material reality. For example, the idea of the authority of the state is a spiritual reality in our mind, yet when statesmen try to change society through the spirit, they do so materially as individuals rather than as the "State" - Henceforth, the state is a spook, a spirit, with material ramifications. Every spiritual thought or thing has material ramifications; Even Engels figured this out in his

Socialism: Utopian and Scientific, when he says, 'A materialistic treatment of history was propounded, and a method found of explaining man's 'knowing' by his 'Being,' instead of, as heretofore, his 'being' by his 'knowing' In other words, when Stirner says, I and the State are enemies, and I have to utilise them both by transforming them into my property, he does not mean this in the sense of idealism but in the sense of materialism. In other words, the egoists have to seize the state as their property not with a mental exercise of consciousness but by physically seizing it as one's own. In other words, we cannot explain the uniqueness by his 'knowing' of the fact that he is unique, but rather, we have to explain the 'Unique' by his 'Owning' - I am only unique when I am an owner; I cannot be unique otherwise. I own myself at all times; therefore, I am unique at all times because, in owning myself, I dispose of myself and recreate myself always in a distinct fashion to my previous self. In my mind I abolish the state as an authority over me, in that I regard it as nothing more than a spook. Then I transform that incorporeal spook into my property, my corporeality; the way I do this is by seizing the material ramifications of that state, the buildings, the resources, the material assets, the connections with individuals, each material individual and so forth. In the same way, if I were to seize the church as my property, I would not be seizing the spiritual realm of it, but rather, the material building. When I consume the eucharist because I am hungry, I consume it as bread but I do not consume the incorporeal body of Christ. Am I free when I abolish the image of Christ from my mind? No; only my mind is free in such a case, my stomach still pangs with the hunger of my egoism. I seize the material communion wafer and satiate my hunger with it. Now, my stomach is free from hunger. Shall I feed my stomach only thoughts of liberation and freedom from spooks? I shall free myself from spooks when they have been transformed into my corporeal property; not when I rid them only through my material brain. The True Egoists retort, "Well, your brain is corporeal, it is your property and hence, you can use your brain to abolish the spooks of the state materially in your mind with material thoughts?" - This would be utter idealistic nonsense. If this were true, then one need only flick his finger and the proletarian revolution would be over by my wishing it to be.

The True Egoists replace "Ownness" with "consciousness," in other words, they are still grappling with Hegelianism. They are still Hegelians and idealists. They do not want to transform the state into their property in the material world, only in their minds, their thought - they think that if they abolish the state as an authority from their mind; then they are free, but in reality, only their mind is free to wreak havoc upon them and to transform their 'True Egoism' into nothing more than yet another spook. The only way for egoism to be a spook is if one's egoism is spearheaded by consciousness, mind and thought rather than by one's material ownership over things and over himself as The Unique. Stirner says the following in regards to the union of egoists, 'You bring into a union your whole power, your competence, and make yourself count; in a society you are employed, with your working power; in the former you live egotistically, in the latter humanly, that is, religiously, as a 'member in the body of this Lord'; to a society you owe what you have, and are in duty bound to it, a.re - possessed by 'social duties'; a union you utilise, and give it up undutifully and unfaithfully when you see no way to use it further. If a society is more than you, then it is more to you than yourself; a union is only your instrument, or the sword with which you sharpen and increase your natural force; the union exists for you and through you, the society conversely lays claim to you for itself and exists even without you; in short, the society is sacred, the union your own; the society consumes you, you consume the union.' When Stirner speaks of this union, he is not merely speaking of a union between me and my own thoughts, but a union between me and my material property towards which I owe nothing. I use it, because it is my property and I give it up when it no longer serves me as a sharp instrument or tool. The union is merely a tool to increase my natural force. That is why, together with my friends, I constructed the Egoist Union International to act as a tool, an instrument with which to sharpen and increase my power upon the world. Now, if I should utilise the union as a natural force in order to seize the state; in order to continue to increase my own natural forces, I can accomplish this as an egoist. Then, because I would no longer have any need of the Idler's State, I can undutifully and unfaithfully give it up when I see no further use for it. When Stirner therefore speaks of the union of egoists, he uses the term 'natural forces,' which means that Stirner's idea of the union of egoists is a materialistic one; not an idealistic one. Henceforth, the argument also goes that when Stirner says that the state and I are enemies, and I annihilate the state by seizing it as my property and replacing it with a union of egoists; he is not talking at all figuratively or metaphorically, he is not talking at all about using his 'consciousness' to seize the state in his mind and annihilate the state in his mind as a spook, rather, he sees that a union with unhuman men can lead to an increase in his natural force needed to seize and annihilate the state; replacing it with a union of egoists rather than a union of unhuman men. The so-called True Egoists do not understand this, if Stirner was speaking about annihilating the state as a spook in the mind then, why didn't he say so? And why is he talking in materialistic terms? Clearly, he meant that the state should be seized and later annihilated materialistically. Those who champion consciousness at the forefront of their egoism have altogether misunderstood Stirner's egoism. Now we ask the 'True Egoists,' in what way did Stirner ask us to seize the welfare of human society characterised by the state? Through the material seizing of the state or the seizing of the state in one's own individual consciousness? And the Union of Egoists that is established, is it a material union among material individuals or merely a union of material individuals thought up by me in my consciousness as a union between me and my mind? Choose, now, either mind shall be the owner or you shall be. The great thing about the 1920's was that everyone was an individualist or an egoist anarchist. Egoism was on everyone's lips during the post-war period and a time of great unemployment during the Great Depression of 1920–1921. Even in the distant lands of Dracula, Romania; in 1923, the Romanian pacifist Eugen Relgis founded the Mi□carea Umanitaristă which progressively became more individualist and egoist. In our modern era with the threat of rapid unemployment, egoism regains the same sort of relevance it had lost a century ago.

II. Conservative, Bourgeois or Communist Egoism

The idlers have always had an unclear role in society. Either a reactionary role or a revolutionary role. This is not merely a phenomenon of the class of idlers, as the proletarians also have been known to have a reactionary role, the so-called labour aristocrats for instance, or as Marx stated in his *Communist Manifesto*, the 'Socialistic bourgeois' who 'want all the advantages of modern social conditions without the struggle and dangers necessarily resulting therefrom. They desire the existing state of society minus its revolutionary and disintegrating elements.' Marx is without a doubt talking about the bourgeoisie and he almost seems to leave the proletariat completely untainted and holy, as if the proletarian class could cause no grievances. Several centuries would prove him wrong when the social democrats in Germany, proletarians themselves, allied against other proletariats, hence, these too became the socialistic bourgeoisie, but came not from the ranks of the bourgeoisie, but from the proletarians.

The idlers in the past have been either reactionary, for example, The Lazzaroni of Naples; or revolutionary, in the case of Sans-culottes of France. The lumpen in modern times are split into two camps: The Lumpenproletariat (petty criminals, vagabonds, homeless etc) and the Lumpen Bourgeoisie (gang leaders and cartel bosses) Throughout the 20th century, the cartel leaders tend to side with the bourgeoisie, while the proletarian counterpart sides with the proletariat in their struggle. The Lazzaroni were staunch supporters of the Monarchy and henceforth, repressed the revolution. These Lazzaroni are diametrically opposed to the Sans-Culottes that were found in France; in that they were intently revolutionary. Yet when Engels wrote about the lumpenproletariat, he only wrote about the Lazzaroni and not about the Sans-culottes who exhibited revolutionary potential.

Henceforth, you had conservative egoists, reactionaries, and bourgeois egoist revolutionaries. The 18th century saw the reactionary Lazzorini in contradiction with the revolutionary Sans-culottes. While the 20th century saw the rise of fascism as the reactionary idlers juxtaposed with the revolutionary illegalist anarchists, anarcho-syndicalists, and anarcho-communists. Anarchism nowadays is a joke, merely merging one ideology with another. Anarchists should realise that they were meant to be idlers and lumpens, they could become revolutionary idlers who, while they actively participate in proletarian revolution, it is only for setting up yet another revolution, the Idler's Revolution immediately afterwards. It was Anarchists who pigeon-holed Stirner into anarchism - now they must take the responsibility as anarchists to lead the Idler's Revolution, to reject communism at the end of the day.

The modern-day fascists attempt to portray themselves as being both reactionaries and revolutionaries at the same time. Is the egoist therefore also a fascist? Not in the slightest. The egoist does not merge the reactionary nature of the idler with the revolutionary nature of the idler in an undialectical or metaphysical manner, in actual fact, the egoist annihilates both the reactionary and revolutionary nature of the idler through a dialectical struggle, and from this struggle, and, with the annihilation of both of these natures, emerges the insurrectionist; and his insurrection which is neither reactionary, nor revolutionary. Henceforth, therein lies a contradiction within the idler that needs to be resolved. The contradiction between reactionary, and revolutionary idlers. The egoist is neither reactionary, nor revolutionary, as Stirner makes clear in *The Unique and Its Property:*

'Revolution and insurrection must not be looked upon as synonymous. The former consists in an overturning of conditions, of the established condition or status, the state or society, and is accordingly a political or social act; the latter has indeed for its unavoidable consequence a transformation of circumstances, yet does not start from it but from men's discontent with themselves, is not an armed rising, but a rising of individuals, a getting up, without regard to the arrangements that spring from it. The revolution aimed at new arrangements; insurrection leads us no longer to let ourselves be arranged, but to arrange ourselves, and sets no glittering hopes on 'institutions.' It is not a fight against the established, since, if it prospers, the established collapses of itself; it is only a working forth of me out of the established. If I leave the established, it is dead and passes into decay. Now, as my object is not the overthrow of an established order but my elevation above it, my purpose and deed are not a political or social but (as directed toward myself and my ownness alone) an egoistic purpose and deed. The revolution commands one to make arrangements, the insurrection [Emporung] demands that he rise or exalt himself. What constitution was to be chosen, this question busied the revolutionary heads, and the whole political period foams with constitutional fights and constitutional questions, as the social talents too were uncommonly inventive in societary arrangements (phalansteries274 and the like). The insurgent strives to become constitutionless.'

In communism, which closely resembles feudalism as we previously discussed, fresh soil is given out by which the idler can emerge and develop himself as an egoist, to become at the end of the day, an insurrectionist; no longer forced to choose a path between revolution or regression. In feudalism in particular, the idler was actually an insurrectionist. The first idler insurrection of major consequence was the Jacquerie. The rural peasants of France were not revolutionaries or reactionaries, but insurrectionists; They destroyed the nobility and looted their wealth as their own property in a way an actual egoist would. It is only with the emergence of capitalism that the idler was forced to choose between a path of reaction or revolution. Communism being the negation of the negation, resembles feudalism in a lot of ways. Henceforth, the Idler's Revolution is another form of Jacquerism; only more evolved, the idler of communism recognizes that he must be a revolutionary before he can be an insurrectionist, lest he should fail like the Jacqueriete.

The Idler's Revolution will also abolish its own revolution at the end. Once the idler becomes an egoist, he ceases to be a revolutionary and becomes an insurrectionist. The Idler's State exists in the Lumpen Phase: the phase between communism and egoism. In this phase, revolution and reaction are in the process of being annihilated along with the board of equity, partitioning and equality, rights, and public property, all are being transformed into the property of the egoist. One might ask, that if the egoist wants to abolish all partitions; then why are they partitioning the means of production themselves? In the same way that socialism has not yet done away with wage-labour, lumpenism has not totally done away with partitioning. This can be described simply as the Lumpen Phase. During this phase, partitioning of the fruits of labour is abolished and replaced by partitioning of the means of production taken by each egoist. When this is done, classes vanish, the state machinery withers away, and partitioning is abolished altogether in all shapes and forms. Free competition of the bourgeoisie and free partitioning of the communist proletarians are annihilated and emerge as Ownness.

Communist egoism is by far the most reactionary form of egoism possible. It still requires me to become subservient, not to God, monarch, to bourgeoisie or nation-states, but to mankind as a whole; communism is by far the most anti-egoist society one can imagine. Communism subverts my uniqueness and transforms me as part of the white herd of sheep; but in this herd of white sheep that I shall find myself as a black sheep, totally unique as I distinguish myself from the masses. One can proclaim to be an 'egoist communist' if he wishes - but this sort of egoism will soon find itself in shambles the moment the idler-proletarian class war disrupts such a communist society. A 'communist egoist' is nothing more than a 'communist' - he is only an egoist where communism is concerned, not a free egoist that entitles himself to everything else beyond the bounds and limits of communism. Those who transform their egoism into a mere suffix of a word delve into a cheap trick of an argument, let me be clearer; a suffix is defined as a group of syllables placed at the end of a word. For example, the word 'dark' in language has content and meaning, but the suffix "ness" which I add to create "darkness" does not take away or add any meaning to the word 'dark,' it merely alters the form of the word to be used in different circumstances. The suffix "ness" only gains meaning when added to another word; so, when some nitwit comes along and says, "I am a "communist egoist" - the only thing that has significance is the word "communist" which has content, while 'egoist' is not treated as a word in itself but merely a suffix which I can add to communism. (And with the reverse, an "egoist communist," communism is rightly being treated as the meaningless suffix, but still an unnecessary suffix, incompatible with egoism.) The suffix of egoism does not alter or change the meaning of communism, it is completely useless and meaningless. Is there any difference between the egoist communist and the plain old communist? There is no difference at all. An egoist communist society is the same as any other communist society, they both intend communism.

Why do the egoist communists feel the need to add this suffix of egoism if it does not at all alter or change the meaning of communism? The answer is rather simple: these folks are not egoists. They are merely communists who, at best, misunderstand egoism as something that can be satiated by voluntarily serving higher power; or at worst, were so bothered by Stirner's critique of socialism that they sought to use his own logic against him so that nothing remains of Stirner's egoism but everything remains of their communism. In other words, twisting Stirner's logic in such a way that is compatible with communism and leaves no room for Stirner "helps them sleep at night." Had they not tried to twist Stirner's logic against him, they would have ended up having to give up communism and become totally dedicated to themselves. If they did this, nothing would remain of communism and everything would remain of Stirner's egoism. So, what is the goal or of these opportunists? Their goal is to reduce their own egoism into nothingness, into a suffix of a word, so that their communism can thrive. Henceforth, because their goal is to reduce their own egoism back into nothing - therefore they are not egoists but in reality, reactionary anti-egoists. There is always a purpose behind why we do things; we must always ask the question, why do these communists also call their communism an egoism; if egoism adds nothing "new" to communism? It is merely a defence mechanism and a way to critique Stirner's egoism. Max Stirner once said, 'Haven't we the priest again there? Who is his God? Man with a capital M! What is the divine? The human! Then the predicate has indeed only been changed into the subject, and, instead of the sentence 'God is love,' they say 'love is divine;' instead of 'God has become man,' - 'man has become God,' etc. It is nothing more or less than a new - religion. Is it too far of the stretch of the imagination, to imagine that Stirner too, would consider egoist communism nothing short of abomination that once again reduces something to a mere predicate?

Quite simply, the egoist communists are those who transform their own egoism into a predicate which is then again changed into a subject. Haven't we become priests again? Who is the God of the Communists? The Masses with a capital M! What is the divine? The Proletariat! Then the predicate has indeed only been changed into the subject. Instead of the sentence, 'The people have become egoists' they say 'the egoists have become the people' and by extension, they have become the masses, the proletariat; the egoist has become a communist. It is the new religion of the Situationist.

Communist egoism was invented in pure form by the Situationist Authors of *The Right To Be Greedy*, who used dialectics in order to subvert Stirner and Marxify him or for a lack of better words, ''Mortify'' him. In other words, they transformed Stirner into a 'narrow egoist' and they transformed themselves into communist egoists using several Hegelian alchemical terms such as *Aufhebung* or the qualitative and quantitative dialectic. In other words, they are communists but they have resurrected Hegelianism using Stirner and Marx. Even the title of their book suggests that the notion of Right has been resurrected. Egoists need to know that when Stirner talked about might as replacing rights, he was mocking, and dialectically inverting Hegel's Elements of the Philosophy of Right; where he critiques not only Hegel's notion of Rights, but also Hegel's notion of freedom and inverts it into Ownness. Stirner had done away with and annihilated freedom and rights using dialectical egoism. Then, however, come the situationists, claiming that they have inverted Stirner! They have not, in actual fact, inverted or annihilated Stirner - instead what they did was resurrect Hegel. Resurrection is not 'inversion.' For instance, Stirner says that feudalism is dead and what was killed cannot return again; but communism is merely a feudalism that has been resurrected, like Christ, under a new glorified body of mankind. The Situationists, as far as we're concerned, have done the same - they have not inverted Stirner's so-called "narrow egoism" into "egoist communism," they have merely resurrected the rights and freedom of Hegel, and consequently, the rights and freedom found in Marx. Many foolish egoists today flock to the situationists because of their seductive message of a communism that is at the same time also egoist. They of course do not flock to egoism - because here we are suggesting that we will destroy the comfort brought about by rights, humanity and communism. The Idler's Manifesto has proven once and for all that egoists can appropriate any dialectic - even those used by these situationists - and use it again against them in a game of tossing yarn to the cat. The communist egoists accuse us of cherry-picking areas of Stirner's book to falsify the notion of the idlers overthrowing the state; we, however, have undertook an in-depth study of Stirner and have supplied multiple quotations from his work as evidence. The communist egoists, who should judge themselves for the same horrendous sin of cherry-picking, have ignored the half of the book where Stirner is critiques communism, and indulged themselves on a small few verses by Stirner in Stirner's Critics, when he remarks that 'Egoism, as Stirner uses it, is not opposed to love nor to thought; it is no enemy of the sweet life of love, nor of devotion and sacrifice; it is no enemy of intimate warmth, but it is also no enemy of critique, nor of socialism, nor, in short, of any actual interest. It doesn't exclude any interest. It is directed against only disinterestedness and the uninteresting; not against love, but against sacred love, not against thought, but against sacred thought, not against socialists, but against sacred socialists, etc.' They take this quotation to mean that Stirner critiqued only sacred socialism; not the materialistic socialism of the anarchists and the Marxists. However, all socialism that was practised in the 20th century, in both the anarchist camp and the Marxist camp was 'sacred.' The only form of non-sacred socialism is when my friend and I share an apartment and split rent, or when friends go camping and decide for a few days to own property in common because it would benefit them at that moment; or any such similar event of individuals freely making use of socialism. What about devotion and sacrifice? Stirner is against sacred love, thought, sacrifice and devotion; but the larger number of thoughts, love, sacrifice and devotion are all sacred. When I see a kid drowning and save him; I do it not because it is the moral thing to do, or the Christian thing, or the human thing to do, but rather, because it pleases me at that moment. The above quotation by Stirner is not against any interest at all - whether it's the socialist interest, bourgeois interest, reactionary interest and so forth - all our egoist interests - even the anarchist interest, the international union of egoist interest and so forth. Stirner is not against any of these interests because he quite clearly states that, in short, he is not against 'any actual interest' - so Stirner would not be against the interest of the Egoist Union International, our interests for that matter. In other words; Stirner is only against disinterestedness, the one who does not care about anything, the absolute nihilist who is not interested in no affair at all. For example; the proletarian who is not interested in anything and simply follows the rules of the communist party because he is a conformist. Stirner is against conformists - even if those conformists are egoists who say, the "international union of egoists" should not happen. All egoists who do not evolve remain static, and want to conform to the old ways of being an egoist at all cost - these are conformists. We are the ever-changing, evolving iconoclasts; we may declare an Internationale of Egoists today and tomorrow we may disband it. For that simple reason, we are always interested in some new interest; we are ever-changing in our interests, and do not hold back when it comes to them. When Stirner said 'I am not against socialism; only sacred socialism,' he precisely meant that he was not against socialism; not that he was or could be in favour of socialism. These modern philosophers of egoist communism do not even understand basic English. If I am not against something; it does not automatically imply that I am staunchly in favour of that something, nor that I am in favour of making it a static goal I place above myself. If I am not against murder; it does mean I advocate and favour murder. If I were to advocate and favour it, I would transform conventional murder into a sacred murder; the same applies to the socialist doctrine. I am not against socialism, but if I advocate and favour an egoist communism, then all I have done is transform socialism into sacred socialism. In other words, all the egoist communists that advocate and favour communism are inherently sacred socialists. The majority of egoist communists are anarchists who claim that Stirner's egoism is compatible with the anarcho-communist ideas of Bakunin or Kropotkin. This false trend of egoism has also become the dominant popular trend of egoism with philosophers such as Samuel Newman and Jacob Blumenfeld. Stirner was never in favour of this egoist communism and declared it to be a hypocrisy. Stirner claims the following:

'The web of hypocrisy of today hangs on the frontiers of two domains, between which our time swings back and forth, attaching its fine threads of deception and self-deception. No longer vigorous enough to serve morality without doubt or weakening, not yet reckless enough to live wholly to egoism, it trembles now toward the one and now toward the other in the spider-web of hypocrisy, and, crippled by the curse of halfness, catches only miserable, stupid flies. 'Here, Stirner critiques the modern trend of egoism and also highlights the trend of deception that was destroying sacred morality. Religion and morality had lost their previous powers, so that in a manner of speaking, humanity still held fast to morality and religion while still committing acts of selfishness, debauchery, and sin etc. This self-deception still exists today: it can be seen in our culture that still clings to humanity. It can also be seen in the threads of deception by the egoist communists who are no longer vigorous enough to serve a proletarian communist morality without doubt or weakness; yet not reckless enough to live wholly according to their egoism and have to attach instead their egoism to the ideas of a proletarian socialist morality. The egoist communists of the situationists are crippled by this curse of the halflings. They catch only the miserable stupid flies and have not produced one single result of bringing this egoist communism into reality since writing their manifesto, 40 years ago. Almost all socialism is a sacred form of socialism, the non-sacred socialism is mostly accidental, unintentional socialism that develops in the context of a union of egoists, amongst friends, and is later dismantled. It is by no means the socialism of Marxists or anarchists. According to Sidney Parker, a form of authoritarian egoism was formulated around the early 20th century; in Parker's essay, Archists, Anarchists, and Egoists, he claims that the first schism between anarchist egoists and authoritarian egoists occurred in a debate between the American egoist Benjamin Tucker and the British egoist Dora Marsden. Tucker himself was a member of the First International, and The Workingmen's Association; later on, however, he would find himself in a primitive First International between Egoists which never fully took shape. It is here that we experience the first egoist schism between 'True German Egoism,' that of John Henry Mackay, and the authoritarian egoism of Marsden. In reality, this schism is a total farce. No egoist should care for what a collective organisation or 'international' thinks, in such a way, 'egoism' has no such thing as schisms, but it does have disagreements between one egoist and another towards their will to power. It would be preferable to have these egoists join hands, so that if the authoritarian egoists fail, the anarchist tradition would take over. The egoist is fluid in their approach and not dogmatic to merely one view of history. If we fail; we will try again, - but we would allow the anarchists within the EUI to try their way, to see if they can succeed, despite our disagreements with them. Marsden expressed her disagreements in regards to the anarchism question: Here is a following excerpt by Sidney Parker:

'The question was answered at some length by Dora Marsden in two essays that appeared in her review for The Egoist September 12, 1914 and February 1, 1915. The first was entitled The Illusion of Anarchism; the second some critics answered. Some months before the appearance of her first essay on anarchism Marsden had been engaged in a controversy with the redoubtable Benjamin Tucker in which she had defended what she called "egoist anarchism" against what she saw as the "clerico-libertarianism" of Tucker. At the premature end of the controversy Tucker denounced her as an "egoist and archist," to which she replied that she was quite willing to "not — according to Mr Tucker — be called "Anarchist" but responded readily to "Egoist."'

According to Sidney Parker, 'In the interval between the end of the controversy and the publication of her first essay she had evidently given considerable thought to the relation of egoism to anarchism and had decided that the latter was something in which she could no longer believe. The gist of her new position was as follows:' and Parker quotes the following from Dora Marsden, where she remarks that:

'An Archist is one who seeks to establish, maintain, and protect by the strongest weapons at his disposal, the law of his own interest' All growing life-forms are aggressive: 'aggressive is what growing means. Each fight for its own place, and to enlarge it, and enlarging it is a growth. And because life-forms are gregarious there are myriads of claims to lay exclusive hold on any place. The claimants are myriad: bird, beast, plant, insect, vermin — each will assert its sole claim to any place as long as it is permitted: as witness the pugnacity of gnat, weed, and flea, the scant ceremony of the housewife's broom, the axe which makes a clearing, the scythe, the fisherman's net, the slaughter- house bludgeon: all assertions of aggressive interest promptly countered by more powerful interests! The world falls to him who can take it, if instinctive action can tell us anything.'

In this, we find the first international split in egoist thought, between the clerical libertarianism of anarchist egoism, and authoritarian egoism which, through its authority, obtains anarchistic freedom for the individual who allows himself the privilege to dominate others. Sidney Parker sees the Marxist communists and the anarchist communists as hypocritical. According to Parker 'Marsden argues that anarchists are among those who, like Christians, seek to muzzle the dominating tendency by urging us to renounce our desires to dominate. Their purpose "is to make men willing to assert that though they are born and inclined archists they ought to be anarchists." Faced with "this colossal encounter of interest", i.e. of lives... the anarchist breaks in with his 'Thus far and no further' and "introduces his 'law' of 'the inviolability of individual liberty'." The anarchist is thus a principled embargoist who sees in domination the evil of evils. "It is the first article of my faith that archistic encroachments upon the 'free' activity of Men are not compatible with the respect due to the dignity of Man as Man. The ideal of Humanity forbids the domination of one man by his fellows... This humanitarian embargo is an Absolute: a procedure of which the observance is Good-in-itself. The government of Man by Man is wrong: the respect of an embargo constitutes Right." The irony is, that in the process of seeking to establish this condition of non-domination called anarchy, the anarchist would be compelled to turn to a sanction that is but another form of domination. In the theoretical society of the anarchist, they would have to resort to the intra-individual domination of conscience in order to prevent the inter-individual domination that characterises political government. In the end, therefore, anarchism boils down to a species of "clerico-libertarianism" and is the gloss covering the wishes of "a unit possessed of the instinct to dominate — even his fellow-men." Not only this, but faced with the practical problems of achieving the "Free Society", the anarchist fantasy would melt away before the realities of power.'

The brave and beautiful spirit, Dora Marsden in particular is one of the greatest authoritarians to ever exist when she continues to explain her definition of Archism in her following work, *The Illusion of Anarchism:*

'[...] Resisting the 'state' because it is the 'state' is therefore futile: a negative, endless, fruitless labor. 'What I want is my state: if I am not able to build it, I do not care whose state is being built: my motivation was and is the establishment of my own.' The world should be shaped according to my wishes, if I could shape it in this way; if I fail, I should not imagine that there should be no world at all: others more powerful than me will take care of it. If I make such a mistake, it is up to me to correct it and pay for it. So, the archist. When the curtain falls on one state, it automatically rises over another. 'The state has fallen, long live the state' - even the widest revolutionary anarchist can't get rid of this. On the morning of his successful revolution, he would have to find means to protect his 'anarchist' ideas: and he would find himself protecting his own interests with all the forces at his disposal, like a vulgar archist: formulating his laws and his state sustained until a freer archist came along to replace and replace him.'

In this quotation alone, she argues that, whether one is an anarchist egoist or authoritarian egoist, the result will still be the state and archism. In other words, the egoist should seize the state, because 'I want my own state' rather than a state that rules over me. Dora Marsden wants to establish her own state as her own property that she can use to mould the world according to her desire as an egoist. Marsden is in full agreement with the proposals of The Idler's Manifesto. The first international schism brought about the end of the first international of egoists and idlers; the egoists are now historically split between the minority archists and the majority anarchists. Whether the revolution is done by one or the other; I do not care. They are both authoritarians in one shape or form. The society of the communists, whether achieved by Marxist or anarchists, is this clerico-libertarianism that is not at all anarchistic but an authority over me. The ultimate question then becomes, would I rather have the cleric libertarian rule over me, or an archist idler who will dissolve the state into my ego? Without a doubt in my ego, I would choose the authoritarian egoist over the communist or anarchist egoist. If both the archist and the anarchist are going to attempt to 'rule over me' in one way or another, why not pick the one that most satisfies my egoist desire, and then utilise them, annihilate either one or the other, in order to replace the archist or the anarchist with the union of egoists.

III. Critical-Utopian Stirnerism and Egoism

The founders of the systems of lumpenism are indeed aware of class antagonism, as well as the action of the decomposing elements, in the prevailing form of society. The idlers, yet in their infancy, offer the spectacle of a class without any historical initiative or any independent political movement. Since the development of industry, the economic situation, as they find it, does not yet offer them the material conditions for the emancipation of the idler. They therefore search after a new science, new social laws that are to create these conditions. They become reformers, they join hands with social democrats to reduce the working week, to reduce it to 4 hours a day through reform, to transform the proletariat into a more idle creature. One such Utopian Idler is the British writer Tom Hodgkinson, who has been the editor of the Idler Magazine since 1993. His writings, for instance, *How to Be Idle: A Loafer's Manifesto* explore the history of the idler's class struggle alongside the proletariat. In his humility, he has written about the idler as a historical social class which under different eras of history were called under different names, lived under different conditions, and came under different contradictions with the other social classes and the mode of production of the time. Tom Hodgkinson, however, did not discover the idler through reading Max Stirner as I did, but through the British critic, man of letters, Dr. Samuel Johnson. Hodgkinson is therefore divorced from the context of Hegel, the Young Hegelians, and Marxism; yet his books, whether he is aware of it or not, are entirely historical, material, and also dialectical. His analysis of important people throughout history is also extraordinary; people of historical importance like the ancient

116

Daoist philosophers, Buddha, Socrates, and Jesus all changed the world by precisely doing nothing and being idle. The list of such people is endless. The problem lies within Hodgkinson's solutions to the idler. His solutions focus on finding better ways by which a person can idle in a capitalist society; through activities such as reading poetry, fishing, writing, cycling and so forth. He is also a petit-bourgeois, similar to the likes of Proudhon, and wants society to go back to the world of small business, instead of imperialist monopoly. He wants to reconstruct society underneath the rulership of the petit-bourgeoisie, small business and the resuscitation from death of the handicraftsman, etc. His books reject class struggle and instead champion creative ways by which an idler can assure his existence within the narrow scope that capitalism allows for the idler's flourishing. One of his books in particular, *The Freedom Manifesto: How to Free Yourself from Anxiety, Fear, Mortgages, Money, Guilt, Debt, Government, Boredom, Supermarkets, Bills, Melancholy, Pain, Depression, Work, and Waste*, rejects both modern machinery and class struggle, and the ideal that a person should use his hands in contract to farmlands instead to in contact with nature; to return to a primitive form of small business, which is the subject of a recent book by him called *Business for Bohemians: Live Well, Make Money*. The title is quite evident of the petit-bourgeois and utopian character of Mr. Hodgkinson. That being said, it is Mr. Hodgkinson who was the first to write about the conditions of the idler class throughout history in a dialectical manner, from the beginning of civilization towards present times, and henceforth, is deserving of our utmost respect for accomplishing this feat; even if Mr. Hodgkinson would be terrified of the solutions presented within The Idler's Manifesto. Hodgkinson has imagined a utopian idler society in which, through petit-bourgeoisie means, everyone owns the means of production for himself and can survive through idle activity one finds enjoyable; In other words, Mr. Hodgkinson is merely another Robert Owen. It was the utopian socialist Robert Owen, the Textile manufacturer and philanthropist, who imagined that the world of socialism could be built through philanthropic acts to construct worker's co-operatives in order to replace the bourgeois capitalist world order. Needless to say, the social experiments of the Owenites had failed. Nowadays, we have utopian idlers like Hodgkinson who want to hand over the means of production to the individual idler through philanthropic acts of the petit-bourgeoisie, to yet again construct small businesses, lands, farms, fishing lakes; ideal property where the idler can develop fully. We of course do not share this Utopian Idlerism which is bound to fail the same way as Owen's Utopian Socialism. Other Utopian idlers have emerged before Mr. Hodgkinson, such as the American writer Bob Black who calls for the Abolition of Labour in his essay *The Abolition of Work*. He gives a short history of idlers throughout the century but not much of the idler's dialectical history. It seems to me that Bob Black wants to abolish only some parts of labour and not labour as a whole. Even though he suggests doing away with most labour through atomizing it, he proclaims that he wants to do some labour for himself. His notion of transforming work into mere play is, in fact, an admirable notion which; even we can adopt. (His idea is presumably supported by the work of anthropologist Marshall Sahlins in his book, *Stone Age Economics; a work of anthropology and early economics*, which, at first glance, also offers a dialectical analysis of the idlers in primitive history. These historical studies of the idlers at different eras are monumental in the cases of both Tom Hodgkinson and Bob Black.) However, his solution is yet again, not without the problems. Black is always stating that, 'We should do away with labour,' but who is this we? Is it capitalist society? Scientists? Labourers themselves? And how exactly are we to do away with labour? Bob Black provides no answer for this. In his essay he urges the workers to simply relax in the parodic phrase, 'Workers of the world… relax!' But Bob Black must take into consideration that, in the capitalist era, the moment a worker relaxes; he starves and dies. As with any other movement of so-called labour abolitionists; these abolitionists are merely the history of the American past haunting these writers and being reborn under new conditions. Black and his followers are merely a reflected moment of history looking back nostalgically at the slave abolitionists movement of the 18th century in America. Bob Black merely applies this abolitionist mentality to the idlers of the world rather than to slaves. The labour abolitionists are the same in character as the slave abolitionists in America. The Bobites wish to abolish labour, but not the conditions and the of production which makes labour possible in the first place! In the same manner, slave abolitionists wanted to liberate slaves but not change the mode of production which made slavery a material reality.

Nay, they would rather become petit-bourgeois, as Bob Black quite clearly shows this characteristic; not only through him being a snitch to the police, but also through his own essay when he said: 'If technology has a role in all this, it is less to automate work out of existence than to open up new realms for re/creation. To some extent we may want to return to handicrafts, which William Morris considered a probable and desirable upshot of communist revolution.'

The petit-bourgeois character and the desire to return to a handicraftsman society is quite self-explanatory in this quote. Black is one of those responsible for favouring the synthesis of Stirner's egoism with the communism found in The Right to be Greedy. Only Paul Lafargue, with his *Right to be Lazy,* deserves our full attention and utmost respect as the only Marxist worth listening to. Alas, even Lafargueists, although revolutionary scientific socialists, are still utopian when it comes to egoism. Lafargue does not attribute revolutionary potential to the class of idlers to abolish labour, but instead attributes this mission to the industrial proletariat. The underdeveloped state of class struggle between idlers and proletarians cause the idlers to consider themselves far superior to all class antagonisms. They want to improve the conditions of idlers by appealing to all members of society, irrespective of their class, and hence, they reject all political and especially all revolutionary action with the peaceful means to achieve these ends, which are necessarily doomed to fail as history has already shown us with the social democrats. These "Egoist Democrats" wish to construct a political party rather than a union of egoists in order to contest in peaceful electoral elections to reduce working hours for the idlers, etc. They are constantly deadening the class struggle of the idler, and are in rejection to the reconciliation of this class's antagonisms. They are constantly dreaming of their realisation of a utopian idler; but with no hopes that this idler be transformed into an egoist. By degrees, they sink deeper into the category of the reactionary conservative egoists. The Hodgkinsonites in England, the Lafargueists in France and the Bobites in America violently oppose all political action on the part of the idler class claiming it is a return of Marx in the guise of egoism. As of late, the egoists, in order to combat this Marxism in the guise of egoism, have taken a deep interest in Stirnerian Economics. For the first time, egoists, rather than focus on Stirner's critique of religion and philosophy, are focusing instead on Stirner's theories of class struggle and economics; the fact that he created a new theory of value due to the result of recreating class struggle anew between the ragamuffin labourers and the lumpen ragamuffin. Stirner's critique of theology goes hand in hand with his critique of political ideology. Stirner sees communism as a mere extension of human theology. Henceforth, Stirner's dialectical critiques of theology and philosophy are also a critique of the political order and of economic theology. However, most Stirnerian economists, few though they are, still do not accept the conclusions of *The Idler's Manifesto*. They have become aware of Stirner's economics, but not to the conclusions which those economic theories will lead. Another recent development in egoist thought occurred at the First Annual Max Stirner Symposium in history sponsored by Duquesne University's Philosophy Department by Cal Nelson in 2023. This symposium "rediscovered" Max Stirner and reclarified The Unique and Its Property to the audience and mostly defended Stirner from critique on various fronts. While they are important in the development of Stirner's thought, they were apologetics of Stirner and focused on redeeming Stirner as if redemption was a concept in which egoists believe in. The symposium was nonetheless most impressive in defending Stirner from various shallow interpretations; that being said, the fellows of this symposium must be aware of not transforming themselves into the 'Young Stirnerites,' in the same manner that the free ones transformed themselves into the 'Young Hegelians.' Not one of these Stirnerians from the symposium talked about Stirner's idea of the idler or the ragamuffin coming into contradiction with the proletarian of communism; not one of them talked about Stirner's dialectics or Stirnerian economy. The symposium was mostly correct about what it had to say in regards to egoism, in regards to Stirner doing away with philosophy and in regards to the redemption of Saint Max from Marx's critique, and the analysis of the human and inhuman dialectic that is transformed into The Unique; however, because the likes of Jacob Blumenfeld do not understand these scientific facts from Stirner, they too are utopian egoists. Blumenfeld in particular is an egoist communist who has misunderstood Stirner; in his book, *All Things are Nothing to Me*, Blumenfeld claims that, 'Only by expropriating what expropriates me, by making the world into my property, is something like communist egoism possible. To Stirner, there is really no difference between saying "the world belongs to everyone" and "the world belongs to me." Communism and egoism are compatible as long as "everyone" is not reified into a new ruling subject above me.' This claim is merely positing a utopian form of egoism where it is compatible with communism in an ideal world. The reason Blumenfeld says this is because the material conditions upon which the Idler's Revolution will be built are still at their infancy; it will become clear to these utopians, once the material conditions are ripe for the full development of the idler, that communism and egoism are incompatible and contradictory. Blumenfeld's book captures the true essence of egoism, and for the most part, Blumenfeld understands Stirner's egoism; for instance, he understands that the dialectic abolishes itself through itself being transformed into the creative nothing. Blumenfeld understands that Stirner commences his book from where Hegel left off; the absolute spirit, and then reveals the truth of the dialectic the creative nothing. However, the domain of this activity is relegated to the activity of consciousness. Many of these authors seem to think that Stirner was of the idea that one can attain freedom simply out of removing spooks from one's mind; henceforth, they become wary that Stirner might be some sort of idealist. They should open their eyes to the section of Stirner's books that critiques communist society, the class and economical struggle between the idler lazy-bones and the proletarian ragamuffin of the future. It is the struggle between these two future classes that shall lead to idleness becoming the new source of value, rather than labour and the dialectic's annihilation of itself into the creative nothing. Stirner, in his critique of communism, is mocking and parodying a chapter in the *Phenomenology of the Spirit* called Lordship and Bondage, in which Hegel argues that the 'Bondsman realised that it is precisely in his work wherein he seemed to have only an alienated existence that he acquires a mind of his own' or that 'Through work, however, the bondsman becomes self–conscious of what he truly is. In the moment which corresponds to desire in the lord's consciousness, it did seem that the aspect of unessential relation to the thing fell to the lot of the bondsman, since in that relation the thing retained its independence.' Henceforth, for Hegel, and likewise Marx, it is out of labour and work that the oppressed gains value for himself in order to topple his lord out of power. Stirner negates Hegel; stating that after communism, it is from the idler, out of his doing nothing, that value is attained for oneself; making it possible for the vagabond to topple the supreme labourer out of power. Stirner talks a long time about the epidemic of overproduction, prices, wages, and communism as the second coming of feudalism; communism as the transformation of labourers into paupers, and ragamuffins, and how we must first become a rag-tag ragamuffin before we can become The Unique. Stirner also talks about how the egoist must seize the state as his own property and how, gradually, it is dialectically transformed into the union of egoists. Far from egoists being told not to cease the state, not to become authoritarians because Stirner wouldn't like that, it is in Stirner that we are urged to seize the state machinery as our property, in order to dissolve it into the union of egoists. These modern Young Stirnernarians seem to forget about these important aspects of

Stirner. For the same reason that Blumenfeld cannot understand Stirner's notions of economics, class struggle and science; Blumenfeld makes an error during his last chapter of *All Things are Nothing to Me: Stirner, Marx, and Communism*, where he seems to think that communism will fulfil Stirner's egoism and egoism will fulfil communism. Where he seems to think the role of the dialectic is to remove any grievances between communism and egoism. Henceforth, most egoists after Stirner, with the exception of a few like Renzo Novatore, are all utopian egoists. The Utopian Egoist differs from the Utopian Idler. The utopian egoists are those who believe, like Hegel did, that consciousness is the means through which one can recognize himself as Unique. It is true that Stiner talks about an egoistic consciousness that is posited against the false consciousness of religiousness, but he also talked about economic conditions that brought about both consciousnesses. Stirner transformed consciousness into a material thing, an object which The Unique owns as his material property; I am owner of my material brain, which, through its processes, is able to arrive at a consciousness of itself as The Unique. In other words, the utopian egoist is he who believes in the power of thought and criticism. It is he who believes that through my thoughts alone, I can dissolve the state in my mind as if it never even existed. This is not at all Stirner's argument! Stirner, in fact, proclaims that he is neither a dogmatist, nor a critic. For the critic always champions the victory of thought; Stirner's Unique and Its Property does not take the critic's role against spooks. Stirner never claimed that the bourgeoisie, the proletariat, social classes, the state, the monarch, only exist in our minds, any egoist who believes this is utopian and idealist. Stirner argued that social classes are made up of singular individuals whose interests seem to coincide; henceforth, the proletarian class is actually not a singular body of people, they do not actually exist as the masses, or as a class, but rather as individuals of flesh and blood who equate the fact that they have similar interests to be one and the same. However, it is clear that from one proletarian and another are not the same being, and their interests, although similar, are not the same interests. Henceforth, Stirner critiques the spook of a class consciousness, that we are conscious as a class. For Stirner we are only conscious of ourselves as individuals whose interests align with other individuals; this is the actual reality. A class therefore, is a collection of individuals whose interests more or less align; it is not, however, a class consciousness with each proletarian being the same as the other. Stirner critiques the parliamentary state in the same way. The parliament is not one unifying body that represents the interests of every single citizen, rather, it is the squabbling of individuals who, with their might and economic power, pretend they represent the interests of the citizen; which is a hollow word, since the citizen himself is also a spook. Stirner is not saying that state, citizen, parliament, proletarian class, bourgeois class, do not exist; he is only saying that the ideas we have about them are flawed, spooked, an illusion. We should rather see the state as egoistic individuals of flesh and blood who use their might against the rest of society. The proletarian and bourgeois class, as individuals, share similar qualities and similar interests. The same applies to the leisure-enjoying idler class. Henceforth, the Utopian Egoist claims that Stirner argues that social classes and government do not exist; while the Scientific Egoist knows that classes and government exist only as individuals whose interests collide. Hence, when the Utopian Egoists talk about abolishing the state, they only think of abolishing the state in their mind and now they are free! Hurrah! The egoist can do whatever he likes! That may be true. But forgive me for being a pessimist; the liberal parliament is still materially there and it will soon abolish your new found freedom by placing you in a prison cell. The Scientific Egoist knows that he has to unite the idlers together under a mutual consensus, to actually annihilate the state, not only in mind but also in physical material action. Yet, we also know that as the egoist, Man is only a quality of me which I own as property; henceforth, my labour, my manhood, my species, my quality as proletarian, idler, communism, anarchist; my consciousness, my thoughts, my reason, and so forth, are only my qualities which do not exhaust everything that I am. Henceforth, when we talk about the ego and that everyone is an egoist. We do not mean this in the absolute sense like Fichte. When we say we are 'Unique,' one can sense that The Unique is universal. The Egoist and Man are one and the same thing; Man is egoist and the egoist is Man. This is not what Stirner's egoism is; rather it is Fichte's absolute egoism. Everyone is unique, but because everyone is unique, everyone is distinctly different and not a universal, such as the concept of Man. When the Utopian Egoists claim that we annihilate society by our mere thinking, by a trick of the mind; I ask you to extend your arm into a campfire and attempt to annihilate the pain of your arm with thought. We will see how well you shall manage. When Stirner says that I and the state are enemies, and that one should utilise it and transform into his physical property, to annihilate the state as state, and the I as I, and replace them with the union of egoists. Do you think Stirner wanted to accomplish this with the power of his mind and thoughts? What union of egoists can he hope to build if he can only annihilate the state and himself through the power of thoughts? The only union he can build is a union between himself and his own thoughts. In other words, the most Hegelian union possible.

The future symposiums on Stirner must beware to be open to reading The Unique and Its Property in a new light once they receive a copy of The Idler's Manifesto, each one of us must keep an open mind to each another, and see whether we will agree or disagree with one other. So far, the symposium seemed to me, a mere echo of the Young Hegelians, but this time, into Young Stirnerian; with Stirner as their master philosopher instead of Hegel. In the same manner that the Young Hegelians were disloyal to Hegel, These Young Stirnerian are disloyal to Stirner; but in a way that, unfortunately, dilutes Stirner and pigeon-holes him into anarchism, communism and so forth.

The only difference as compared with the old, outspoken slavery is this, that the worker of a communist society seems to be free because he is not sold once and for all; neither is he sold as a piecemeal under the pretence of a free contract between employer and employee. But rather the worker of a communist society has no choice but to give himself freely as a man for the entirety of his life towards the wellbeing of society, but he is forced to give himself in this way instead, being slave to no particular person, not even the slave a whole property-holding class but rather a slave to an even greater master - the whole of property-holding communist society itself. The more society advances forward towards communism, the more enslaved man becomes by an even more invisible, subtle and larger entity than the previous one. First, Man is enslaved by an individual in feudalism; then by the whole property-holding class in capitalism and finally by the whole of society in communism. It was in this manner also in which Max Stirner so vehemently attacked the idea of communism. When he critiqued communism by stating, 'Let us then do away with personal property. 'Let no one haye anything any longer, let everyone be a - ragamuffin. Let property be impersonal, let it belong to - society' In other words, communism merely enslaves us under a new even more impersonal and subtle force. Therefore communism cannot possibly be an egoism. We need to wait a few years to separate the wheat from the chaff, the wisdom from the garbage, these Young Stirnerian will supply us with.

4. POSITION OF THE IDLERS IN RELATION TO THE VARIOUS EXISTING OPPOSITION PARTIES

It may be the case that the Automative Revolution is the spark by which the coming proletarian revolution is triggered. Henceforth, it is reasonable to assume that the idlers might come into existence, not out of their direct relation to the serf-proletariat, but by the Automative Revolution running wild and free during the capitalist era; transforming each industrial proletariat into an idler. The remaining industrial proletariat will construct new proletarian parties, and the idlers will be forced to construct their own parties ahead of schedule. The idlers might have several parties; some might be Idler-Democratic parties: these are reformists, those who seek reform out of the poverty of automationization, who wants to empower Universal Basic Income for the idlers, to seek a more comfortable reality of idlers living in an automated capitalist era.

Proletarian revolutions of the world yet to come might ignite in semi-feudal countries such as India, Peru, Philippines and Turkey. A revolution in each of these would ignite other revolutions of adjacent countries, for instance, the one in India might spark a secondary revolution against the state capitalism of China's communist party, to restore it to the principles of Marxism-Leninism-Maoism. Yet, these semi-feudal revolutions are merely revolutions that harken back to the 20th century past of the industrial revolution. They are the last proletarian revolutions that have the general character of allying the industrial proletariat with feudal peasants. These last few revolutions will, once and for all, put an end to all feudal elements within bourgeois society. The death of the peasantry makes more room for the social class of the future. The most potent revolutions are those that occur because of the conditions of the developing Automative Revolution, with solely the industrial proletariat leading the struggle. The alliance of the industrial proletariat and the peasantry will be replaced with an alliance between the industrial proletariat and the idlers; with the proletariat as leaders of this struggle against the bourgeoisie. As I remarked before, the idlers will be forced to fight against the enemy of its enemy, namely the bourgeoisie. However, as Iago, in the Shakespearian play Othello, said, 'I follow him to serve my turn upon him' In the same manner, the idlers follow the communist revolution only for it to be followed by a subsequent Revolution of the Idlers themselves. I can be friends with the proletarians and aid them in their revolution at first without proclaiming myself as an egoist; as the egoist saying goes, 'If you have a friend; keep her as such and do not tell her your secrets much. For, if that friend becomes your foe; out into the world your secrets go.' - A fool who spouts all his secrets to his friend has the Sword of Damocles hanging over their head at all times. Some may say Alexander Hope is a liar - that he attempts to become subversive of everything and mix up egoism with authoritarianism in order seize power for himself through the state. However, it is not a lie but merely my studies of Stirner that have led me to this conclusion. If, however, I am a liar in giving out what I think is the spooky truth, then I agree with the great poet William Blake who proclaims, 'A truth that's told with bad intent beats all the lies you can invent.' Isn't it the egoist thing to do to seek power for myself, even if it includes the desire to seize the state for myself tomorrow? The struggle commences now, in the era of imperialist capitalism. The Automative Revolution will make our path clear. Yet, because we are still in capitalism, even if there is an Automative Revolution, the idler still has an unclear role. He may be a reactionary or a revolutionary. If the modern lumpen become reactionary, they are no different from fascist Italy and Nazi Germany. In other words, they are not egoists. These are no friends of ours. All fascism develops as a desire to do away with rapid unemployment. In Britain, Oswald Mosley's Union of Fascists developed as a consequence to the problem of the unemployed. Hitler and Mussolini had gotten rid of unemployment in a matter of a few months.; they transformed the lumpenproletariat into the proletariat by force. In Germany, by 1930, the spectre of unemployment and of wage cuts haunted virtually every German citizen, bringing fear into the stoutest worker's heart. Resistance to dictatorship was impossible when that meant starvation and joblessness. The unemployment of the industrial revolution brought about Mussolini and Hitler; what shall the Automative Revolution bring? With the approach of the Automaton Revolution, the worst crisis of unemployment in all of history, the most horrid fascism shall develop in our midst. The idler is the eternal enemy of the fascist; the fascists desire to transform the lumpen back into the proletariat, while the idlers seek the opposite; namely the transformation of the proletarians into the ranks of the lumpen. The idlers wish to elevate the idler in power; through this, the idler can become an egoist - a creator and leisure-enjoyer at the same time. While the fascist preaches the motto "Everything in the State, nothing outside the State, nothing against the State" The Egoist has the opposite motto "Everything in me, nothing outside of me, nothing against me" - that is to say that society and the state are in me as property and not as things that lord over me. We need not wait for the perfect conditions of communism, for a stateless, classless, and moneyless society. The Automative Revolution will see to it that the lumpen-proletariat are strong enough to help the proletarians win their communist revolution and establish the dictatorship of the proletariat. Now… need we wait for the dictatorship of the proletariat to transition into communism? Not necessarily, if the lumpen are strong enough, perhaps they can seize the moment, immediately launch another revolution against the dictatorship of the proletariat, and seize its state machinery in order to transition into the union of egoists as quickly as possible. However, the best way to win this revolution is to wait for the socialists to transition into communism. A stateless, classless, moneyless society: such a society would allow for the full development of the idler class. Both options are viable. Which option is the best one? The best option will become clear as the Automaton Revolution continues to ravage industry. What about a third option? The third option would be a mechanical, barbaric action rather than dialectical means. We already find ourselves in a war between Ukraine and Russia. The conclusion of this war will be a disaster no matter who is the victor. If Russia loses this war, we'd see fascists take power in that country worse than the fascist oligarchy that is in power as of now. One can speculate on the victor; however, based on NATO's backing of Ukraine and the lack of financial and militaristic resources of Russia, one starts to speculate a Ukrainian victory even though at first, the victor of the war was expected to be Russia. America's lips are whispering of a second civil war. A weak America is susceptible to its enemies who seek to take advantage of this development. We shall see what developments the United States takes after the elections of 2024. The weakening of America would result in Russia taking the most predictable action; further war might lead to nuclear war. Russia might attack first; it currently has more reasons to use nuclear weapons than any other country in the world at this moment in time. Billions of lives might be lost if World War III breaks out; however, even if the world suffers nuclear devastation, the egoist will thrive in this barbaric civilization where the war of all against all is complete. The union of egoists will thrive in such a world of warriors and barbarians. But let us not be pessimistic, it is preferable for the egoist to become an aristocrat rather than a barbaric warrior. The idlers must turn their attention chiefly to Germany, because that country is on the eve of a proletarian revolution that is bound to be carried out under more advanced automated conditions of European civilization. Germany is on the forefront of the Automative Revolution, it is the leading country when it comes to robotics, cybernetics and automatons. Followed by other countries in the following chronological order: Japan, South Korea, United States, and China. These countries will increase the influx of the lumpen-proletariat, the idlers of tomorrow. At the same time, the conditions of the proletarians will worsen to the extent that there will be massive unemployment and poverty even if policies such as the universal basic income are brought forward as a safety-net. Conditions for the industrial proletariat will worsen until they bring about another proletarian revolution in Germany which is merely a prelude to the immediately following Idler's Revolution. In short, idlers everywhere support every revolutionary movement against the existing social and political order of things. In all these movements, they bring to the front, as the leading question in each, the property question; no matter what its degree of development at the time. The idlers disdain to conceal their views and aims. They openly declare that their ends can be attained only by the forcible overthrow of all existing social conditions. Let the ruling classes tremble at an Idler's Revolution. The idlers have nothing to lose but their ghosts.

IDLERS OF ALL COUNTRIES, UNITE!

www.ingramcontent.com/pod-product-compliance
Lightning Source LLC
Chambersburg PA
CBHW031304250726
48656CB00005B/1626